TO:

Logan

FROM:

Mom

DATE:

4-9-22

Logan

[illegible]

11-9-99

HOW FAR YOU HAVE COME

MUSINGS ON BEAUTY AND COURAGE

MORGAN HARPER NICHOLS

TABLE OF CONTENTS

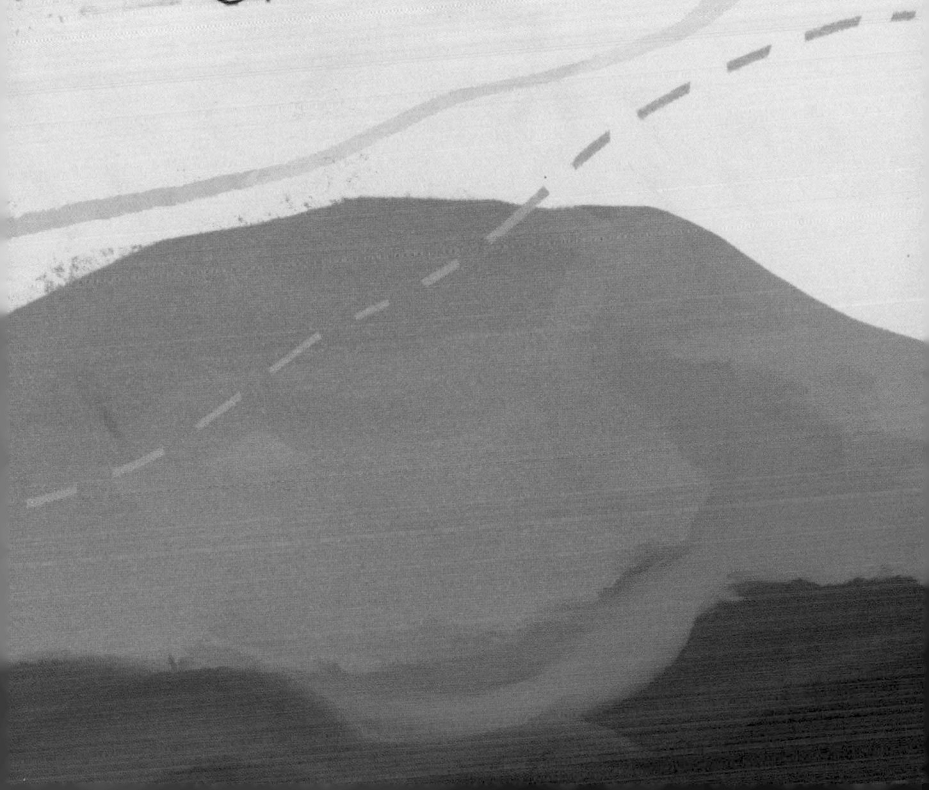

ZONDERVAN

How Far You Have Come

Copyright © 2021 by Novkoa, LLC

Requests for information should be addressed to:
Zondervan, *3900 Sparks Dr. SE, Grand Rapids, Michigan 49546*

ISBN 978-0-310-45659-9 (hardcover)
ISBN 978-0-310-45685-8 (audio)
ISBN 978-0-310-45655-1 (ebook)

Zondervan titles may be purchased in bulk for educational, business, fundraising, or sales promotional use. For information, please email SpecialMarkets@Zondervan.com.

Art direction: Tiffany Forrester
Cover Illustration: Morgan Harper Nichols
Interior Illustrations: Morgan Harper Nichols
Interior Design: Mallory Collins

Printed in Canada

21 22 23 24 25   FR   10 9 8 7 6 5 4 3 2

INTRODUCTION

In the summer of 1996, when I was six years old, I took a road trip with my family from Atlanta, Georgia, to Los Angeles, California. To the outside observer, it was a standard family trip. We were going to visit relatives, and my dad, a pastor, was going to preach. Little did I know, this was the seminal moment of an ongoing journey of personal growth. For the next twenty years of my life, I would end up traveling these eight state lines many times for many reasons. From east to west and back again, I would end up discovering that so many of the moments I thought I was just passing through, I was on the verge of learning something new. Here on the road, I was growing into who I was meant to be.

As I've traveled, I've often looked to the natural influences that surround me to become the metaphor for my story. On every landscape I have set foot on, both the fallenness and holiness remind me of how beautifully diverse and complex our world is. It's no wonder there's a long-standing literary tradition of looking to the natural world to communicate our emotional and spiritual experiences. To reflect on our lives, we must look outside ourselves. The mountains and the plains and everything in between have been a great gift to my soul, and I believe they can be a great gift to you too.

From lessons on friendships to humbling career failures to wrestling with hard histories while searching for a future, I am just one of many who have learned that the journey has a way of shaping us and awakening us. Whenever I return to the road, I measure how far I've come, and I am free to reflect upon and reinvent the woman I want to be. This book is an ode to personal growth—a celebration of the lifelong process of becoming. Here's a collection of stories from a well-traveled path, and the art and poetry I found along the way.

THIS ROAD HOLDS OUR MEMORY—
THE STORIES OF TRAVELERS
IN BETWEEN
THEIR DREAMS
AND THEIR DOUBTS.

WE HEAD WEST ALONG
THIS FAITHFUL PATH
TO START AGAIN,
HOPING WHAT WE'RE SEARCHING FOR
IS JUST OVER THE HORIZON.

SHE LAUGHS BECAUSE SHE KNOWS
WE WILL NOT FIND
ON THE OTHER SIDE.

OH NO, WHAT WE'RE LOOKING FOR?
WE FIND AS WE GO.

KEEP GOING,
KEEP GOING,
LET THE SKIES SURPRISE YOU.
EVEN WHEN STORM WATER CLAMORS
AND THE WINDS WRECK YOUR SHORES,
YOU ARE FREE TO START AGAIN.
YOU ARE FREE TO START AGAIN.

FOR IN THIS LIFE THERE WILL BE MANY ROADS
WE DO NOT TAKE,
AND ON SOME MORNINGS, WE WAKE
AND FIND
THERE ARE BRIGHT-ORANGE BARRICADES
CLOSING OFF ENTRYWAYS
AND BRIDGES, LAKES, AND CITYSCAPES
WE LONG TO GO AND SEE.

WE HAVE A DUTY TO FOCUS
ON THE ROAD BEFORE US—
TO DREAM OF THE DESTINATION
BUT NEVER FORGET
TO DELIGHT IN THE DRIVE.

RECORD YOUR MOTHER'S LAUGHTER
IN YOUR MIND,
THE SECRET SIBLING HANDSHAKES
AND DAD'S KNOWING SIGHS.

THIS IS THE FUEL YOU'LL NEED
TO JOURNEY WIDE.

Invite the breeze in—
windows down.
Hear the sound of other wheels
cycling over the ground.
Let the air kiss your cheeks,
and though no one looks
and no one speaks,
you are never alone
out here on the road,
this collective in-between.

You tap your fingers along the dashboard.

Detour.

As the hours go on,
street lamps glare into your eyes
as they fight against
the approaching night sky.

Red taillights.

You have followed the signs,
but the map in your mind
tells you this is not the way.

You realize there is a way back,
but it will take a little longer now.
Exit.
Turn around.
Try again.

Refill your tank, turn the key.
Oh, how good it is to drive
and just keep trying.

In the long stretches of wilderness,
without street lamps to guide you,
your sight narrows, unreliable.

There is nothing for miles.
Your head is spinning
faster than the wheels treading earth beneath you.

But beyond your headlights
the moon still shines above you,
and the earth is still steady,
spinning on her axis
as she did yesterday and the day before
and before that.

Here you are
all alone,

but more connected than you think.

The forest is thriving,
the trees are talking,
cicadas roaring,
foxes humming,

enjoy their song.

Keep traveling
to where the wilderness is unraveling.

Listen,
and let the rhythms of this place
bear the weight of your heavy mind.

IN THIS LIFE
YOU WILL FIND BRIDGES,
TRAILS WELL-WORN AND BROKEN
UNPAVED AND ABUNDANTLY CLEAR
MANY OTHERS HAVE TRAVELED HERE.

YOU WILL MEET OTHER
TRAVELERS ON TRAILS
LEAVING FOOTPRINTS OF ALL SIZES.
AND MANY WILL FORGET
TO SLOW DOWN
AND REFLECT
ON ALL IT TOOK TO GET HERE—
THE STRENGTH,
STRUGGLE,
PROGRESS.

SEE YOUR LIFE WITH
GRATITUDE,
JOY AND PEACE.
INVITE OTHERS TO
JOIN YOUR MOVEMENT
OF INTENTIONALITY.

9

My heart wanders above the pines into
the arctic sky,
where I can see their peaks
through white clouds,
and I rush down to see
their roots stretching out
into turquoise water.

I hover above the tangled summer grass
whose strands braid together
over the soil
protecting it, safe here.

I remember the stagnant water
a few yards behind,
leaves floating in abandon,
detached.

I blink and I blink and I blink
and with my eyelids' next rapid opening,
I see before me
flickers of red, yellow, and green,
the slow-burning July beam
of night-flying
soft-bodied beetles
emerging from their homes
beneath the trees,
luminescent,
shining
as they are
not moving very far
away from this low land,
glimmers of lightning
enlightening
right here
where I stand.

The summer of July 1996, Atlanta, Georgia. I awoke at the break of day just in time to see the clouds coming down to touch the earth. I snuck out to the porch and watched the squirrels dance in the trees before the heat set in. I had never been an early riser, but on this day I awoke at the sun's rise to watch my parents hauling our suitcases into the trunk of the Volvo. Today was the day. We were heading back to California for the first time since I was a toddler.

I spent the first two years of my life in California, and although my memories were foggy, I desperately wanted to return. I clung to my faint memory of the blue Los Angeles ocean air, and I dreamt of the olive-green leaves of the palm trees waving in the wind. Even at six years old, I had a deep sense that this was the place where my heart belonged, and finally, finally, we were headed back, even if for just a short visit.

My heart raced as I paced through the morning mist. I placed my neon sunglasses on my face. Their yellow and pink frames always reminded me of California sunsets.

"Can we leave now?" I asked.

My parents didn't even hear my question, focused on lugging our bags to the car, diving in and out of the house like birds flying to and fro from their nests. Water bottles, Band-Aids, magazines, cassette tapes, lotions. Did we really need all of this? My sister and I had already packed our coloring books, crayons, black-and-white composition notebooks, and fanny

packs stuffed with friendship-bracelet beads and Polly Pocket dolls. *We* had everything we needed. What was taking them so long?

I wasn't the only one in a rush. The entire city was abuzz with anticipation. The summer Olympics were taking place just a few miles away in the center of the city, and it had been the sole topic of conversation around the dinner table for months. We'd watch the news each night to hear endless reporting about the upcoming festivities and events. Whenever we'd drive through downtown Atlanta, we'd see roads closed and construction taking place to accommodate the massive event. We couldn't even go see the laser show at Stone Mountain Park because there was

a cycling race happening there. I was slowly beginning to understand that this sporting event was a big deal.

But honestly, I didn't care. All I could think about was California—its cliché images of palm trees blowing in the wind and Disney characters walking the streets of Hollywood. Surely we could simply watch the Olympics on TV, right? I was becoming obsessed with heading west, and I knew I couldn't rest until I heard the sound of that Volvo's engine. We had 2,100 miles to go, and we were still at ground zero.

My anxious thoughts swelled as the sun crawled higher and higher to the center of the sky. I flopped down on the edge of the front porch. Six years old and nothing to do but fidget and wait.

I couldn't sit still any longer. I began hopping from one porch board to the next as I counted. *Five, ten, fifteen, twenty,*

twenty-five . . . I'd lose track and start again. *Five, ten* . . . I felt like every hop I made added five more minutes to the clock. The sun was shining brightly overhead, and its beams started casting shadows in the opposite direction. This was a big day, and I already felt like it was getting away.

"Okay, kids, let's go."

I darted toward the car and snapped my seatbelt in place before my mother could even finish her thought. I restlessly set my gaze outside the window toward the dazzling asphalt, watching for the first indication of Georgia's hot earth rolling behind me. I positioned my crayons and colored pencils at the ready and set my fanny pack with care on the armrest.

Tonight. We could be halfway to California by tonight.

My dad fired up the engine, and we began our journey to the interstate. I looked down at my wrist and noticed my watch was missing, but I wasn't too concerned. My mind was moving too fast for the second hand anyway. Time could not contain me.

But of course, I was six, so I couldn't help myself. I looked at the clock on the Volvo's dashboard.

"Is that the right time?"

"Yep, that's right!" Dad replied.

I gasped in disbelief. It was nearly five o'clock! Where had the day gone? There was no way we would be in Texas by that evening, not even with the aid of time zones. I was practically a math expert at this point, after spending the whole day on the front porch counting my way to a million and back. I dropped my shoulders and sunk my chin into the palm of my hand, fixing my eyes outside the window. The sun would set soon, and all I could think about was how we were miserably behind. This was not my plan.

Sulking in my seat, I stared out the window and looked at

the signs marked "Atlanta." What a disappointment. It seemed we were making no progress at all! I had seen these streets on the TV a few nights previous, and I knew we were getting close to the hub of the big games. Traffic stalled as we neared the place where the famous Olympic torch had ignited the sky like fireworks for the first time a few nights ago. *Ugh,* I thought. *Another delay.*

I looked out the window to see a twenty-story mural painted with faces of people from around the world on the side of a hotel lining the interstate. Apricot. Sepia. Bronze. Gold. Earth tone. Sienna. It seemed like every color my crayon box could hold was used to create that mural, plus a thousand more. For the first time all day, I slowed my thoughts and tuned in to the world

right before me. I had never seen a canvas big enough to hold every color God created, but I think this mural may have captured all of them. I looked at the faces, some young, some wrinkled. A multitude of people painted on this wall. I took off my sunglasses but quickly replaced them, realizing how they magically transformed the world into richer tones.

Just beyond the mural I saw the 116-foot silver tower holding the cauldron for the Olympic torch. Bystanders flooded the bridge that stretched toward the tower. They huddled close, holding their cameras and backpacks, all while wrangling their kids so they didn't get lost in the masses. All roads pointed here, to Atlanta, to gather around this roaring light. The globe came together for a moment to celebrate every nation around the world. The people pressed against one another on that bridge captivated my attention and stirred my sulking spirit. Time froze as I watched them. I witnessed the world existing in light together—a universal expression of pride right in my backyard.

As we were parked there on the highway, I realized that perhaps this was how it was meant to be. If we had left when my heart desired, we would have missed this clamoring scene. The whole world was right here in Georgia, and I almost missed this scene of beauty because I was too busy racing toward the next one. And even though we caught only a glimpse of the torch's fire on the bridge, it changed me. I felt connected to something bigger than the tick of the clock. I looked to my left, and I noticed my sister with the same wonder on her face too.

What a gift it was to be inconvenienced. When we are, we always have the choice to look, listen, and delight in the beauty that is before us. We have to train ourselves to look for light and hope, no matter if we're moving at our preferred pace or not. Not an easy lesson for a six-year-old, but somehow it seeped in. I was where I was meant to be, even when I thought I should be somewhere else by then.

The Volvo started to pick up more speed now, and I took one last look out the back window at the bridge, the tower, and the mural. I imagined how the midnight sky would be lit by the torch's magnificence tonight. I almost asked Dad if we could stay, but I stopped just short of it. *No*, I thought. *Enjoy the moment as it unfolds, nothing more, nothing less.*

Time was ticking, but it was not ticking against us. I didn't need to rush, but rather, look and listen. Take the day in, and always wear sunglasses.

May your hope be as bright
as flaming light
held high along the unknown shores of night.
May you never lose the vision
of what the years to come could be,
and no matter how dark the sea may look,
you have the courage within
to dream.

And if your raging fire
dwindles down to a flickering flame,
barely burning now,
a victim of the sea's windy rage,
do not let go,
for Hope has not let go of you.
Hold on with all you have
to the Light that conquers blue.

WE ALL COME AND GO
NO ONE HERE FOREVER,
BUT WE ARE WOVEN INTO
THE STORIES OF
THOSE BEFORE
AND BEHIND US.

WE FOLLOW ONE ANOTHER
ON WELL-CARVED PATHS,
AND AT THE CENTER
OF OUR CIRCLE
THERE IS GRACE,
AND WE HEAR IT SAY,
"CARRY ON IN
THIS RACE,
LEAVE NO ONE
BEHIND."

INVITE JOY TO
MEET YOUR SORROW.
LET IN HOPE
FOR TOMORROW.
BRIDGE THE FRAGMENTS
OF WHO YOU ARE,
AND LEARN TO SEE
BEAUTY IN YOUR SCARS.

IMAGINE THE TABLE
DESIGNED TO SEAT

THE FAMILY YOU HAVE KNOWN
AND LONG TO MEET.
INVITE THE STRANGER,
AND LEARN HIS STORY, TOO.
BE THE BRIDGE TO ALL
THESE PERSONS PASSING THROUGH.

BECAUSE IN LOVE,
THERE WILL BE ROOM
FOR EACH AND EVERY ONE OF US.
AND IN LOVE THERE IS
ROOM FOR ALL OF YOU.

You will desire to go
beyond the limits
to get there faster.

But moving at a careful pace
requires courage in this race,
as if to say

time does not define me,
I do not answer to the tick of the clock
and will not give in to its alluring tongue.

In my own speed,
with my own limits,
I am still becoming.

WHEN YOU LOOK AT THE MAP
AND TRACE YOUR FINGER OVER
HUNDREDS OF ROUTES
YOU WILL FIND NO FINISH LINE.

ONE PATH LEADS TO ANOTHER,
SOME DWINDLE TO DEAD ENDS,
SOME ORDERLY ON GRIDS,
AND OTHERS TWISTING
AROUND THE RIDGE.

ALL TOGETHER THEY CREATE
OUR FAMILY RECORD.
OUR TIMES, OUR PLACES,
A STORY OF
UNRUSHED
TRAVELERS
PUSHING FORWARD
AT THEIR OWN PACES

A tiny burst of fire
burning brightly
in the sky.
I cannot reach her but my hand
stretches upward,
and I try
to make sense
of the miracle
held by gravity
in space.
I am in awe and
mystified that I cannot see
her face.
I wish I knew
what God named her
and why she sits so close
to earth,
perhaps a miracle to arrest
my wonder
and remind me
of my worth.

Your heart burns red
at dead ends,
and yet, you trust that there is a way forward,
because you've been here before,
and you know you can start again.

Look past the stop signs to the beauty just beyond.
Look how earth's clay painted red
meets the orange brushstrokes of the sky.
What if this view is all for you?
And what if you are better for it?

Go back.
Try again.
And again.
And again, and tell your heart,
you will not miss out on what was meant for you.

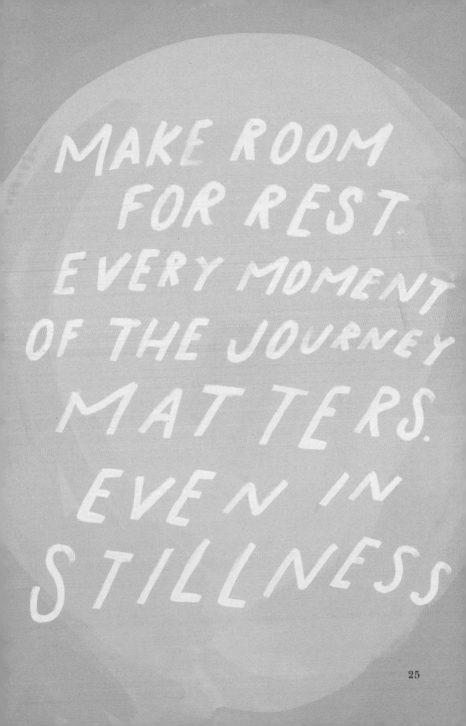

MAKE ROOM FOR REST. EVERY MOMENT OF THE JOURNEY MATTERS. EVEN IN STILLNESS

I WILL NOT LET
THE PULSE
OF THE CLOCK
DICTATE THE
PULSE OF
MY LIFE

The sienna color
clay of childhood play,
and five miles of birds
on powerlines, planes
rushing and roaring
in the sky,
summer steam
clinging to
my skin.

Oh, how could
I ever leave it
behind?

And oh,
I know
I must.

The red cedars
glowing green
teach us
it is okay to just be.
There is no need
to rush.
This moment
right here
is enough.

One hundred pines
stand shoulder to shoulder,
grow older,
and bolder
because they know they have each other.

Rooted to one another,
we grow taller.

We are freest in love.

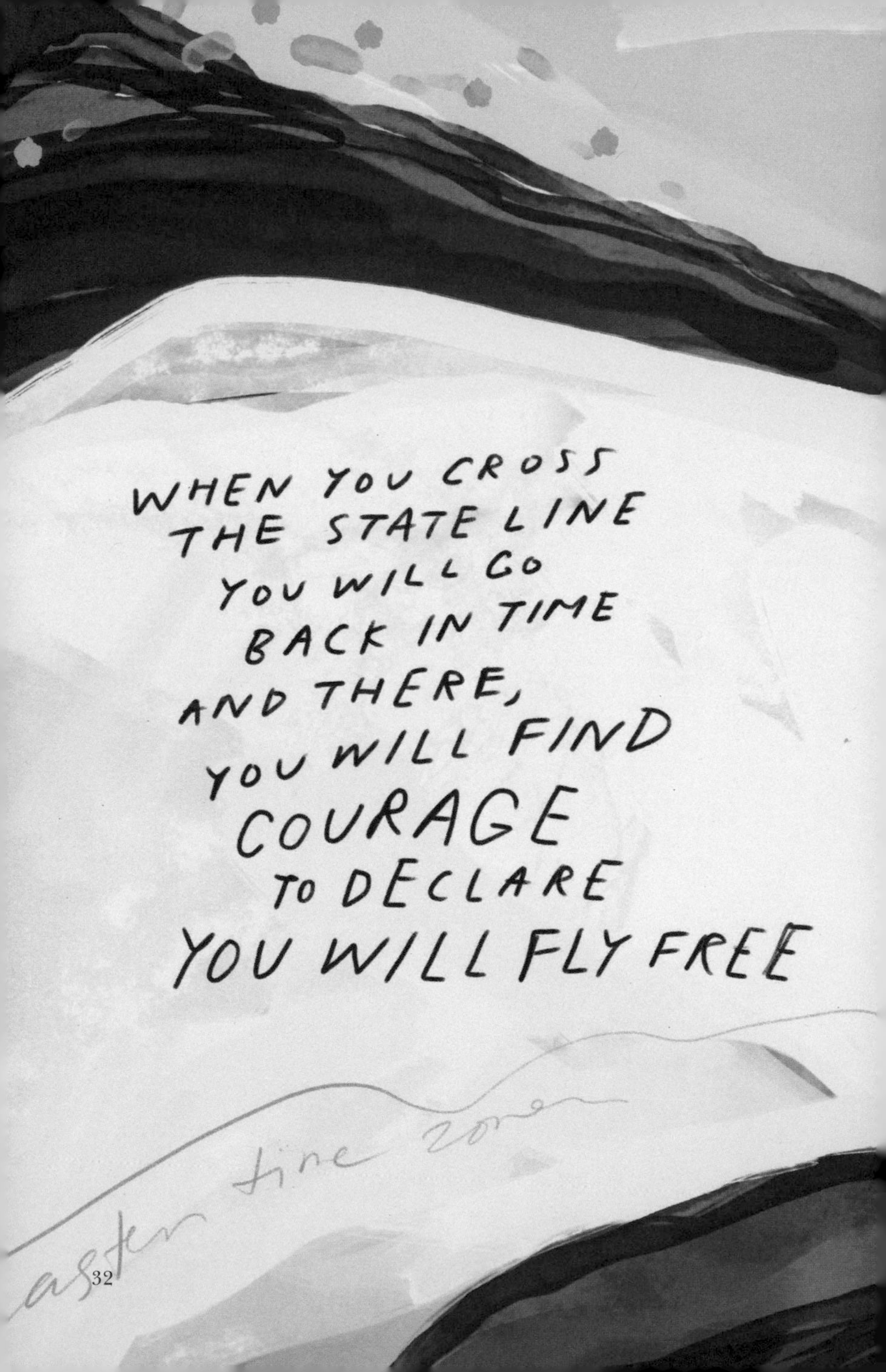

WHEN YOU CROSS
THE STATE LINE
YOU WILL GO
BACK IN TIME
AND THERE,
YOU WILL FIND
COURAGE
TO DECLARE
YOU WILL FLY FREE

eastern time zone

WITHOUT KNOWING
WHAT COMES NEXT,
YOU ARE STILL
FLYING WEST.
AND EVEN THE SMALLEST STEPS
ARE MARKED BY
COURAGE
AND GRACE

Morning dew is frozen over
as winter hints at her arrival.
Your jacket shields against the wind,
and bitter coffee
lingers in your mouth,
while your mind turns gray,
as exhausted as these overcast skies.

You fear you cannot face today,
but perhaps you have strength
to carry on another minute,
six sets of ten seconds.
Maybe you'll lose track of them
living
one moment at a time.

These days are tiring,
but hope is hovering.

PERHAPS THERE IS BEAUTY
YET TO BE REVEALED,
   AND SOME OF THE
RICHEST BLUES I WILL EVER KNOW
   WILL COME FROM WANDERING,
TRUSTING.
   IT'S OKAY TO HAVE MY PLANS
WHILE HOLDING THEM LOOSELY
IN MY HANDS.

   CUPPING WATER IN MY PALM,
IT'S ALREADY SLIPPING
   THROUGH MY FINGERS.
THE WHOLE EXPERIENCE IS GONE
BEFORE I CAN EVEN TASTE IT,
AND I LEAVE EMPTY-HANDED,
YET CHANGED BY THE BLUE.

Step into these grassy farmlands,
take cold air in, let your lungs expand.
In morning's mist, shed your fears and run
free to pursue all the dreams you planned.

Learn to feel the yellow grass beneath your feet.
Learn to keep going, even when it's hard.
And when you need to, take a breath to rest and
learn to be present right where you are.

The days ahead will not be easy,
you will dive into waters unknown.
You will listen for your name in crowded spaces.
Unnoticed, you will feel like you'll never find your home.

Listen to the story of the grass beneath your feet.
Shout your name louder than ever before.
Your journey may have acres of confusion,
but for every step you take, your wisdom will grow all the more.

I DO NOT KNOW WHY I AM STILL HERE
OR WHY I SAY ANYTHING AT ALL.

IN A WORLD SPINNING WILDLY WITH QUESTIONS
WATER CIRCLING IN A THOUSAND DIRECTIONS,
MY TIRED HEART STILL BEATS
WHILE I SEARCH FOR MEANING,
AND I FEEL LIKE AN IMPOSTER
ON SOME HERO'S JOURNEY.

I WILL TRUST THAT I MATTER.
I AM HERE,
I LIVE,
I BREATHE,
AND I SPEAK WITH CURIOSITY.

EXISTENCE IS A MYSTERY,
BUT I WILL LIVE MY LIFE
WITH INTENTION.

I wonder
if the blackbird
carries tales
of times she tried and failed
or if she has always taken flight
with such ease and grace.
I wonder if she struggles to find her place,
where to put her nest.
I call out to her as she flies by,
but she doesn't bat an eye.
She is focused,
fierce,
too busy living free
to have time to explain all her ways to me.
So instead of watching, waiting,
and being left behind,
I decided to breathe deep
and try flying too.

WHEN YOU'RE OVERWHELMED BY
RESPONSIBILITIES
AND THE WAY
OTHERS SEE YOU,
MAY YOU KNOW
YOU DO NOT NEED TO
EXPLAIN YOURSELF

YOU WERE MADE FOR
DEEPER WATERS
WHERE EXPECTATIONS
ARE WASHED AWAY
TO REVEAL YOUR WORTH WITHIN
YOU HOLD A RESERVOIR OF LOVE.
THE UNDER CURRENT
OF YOUR
EVERY DAY.

Break the binds
of books,
and the ways you used to think.
Take a closer look.
Your heart is calling you onward.

Come and sit by the window.
Consider the glass with its
smudges and fingerprints.
Consider what's beyond
and where you belong.
Talk to yourself
and all the women and men
who came before
who write to you
secrets,

secrets that can harm you,
secrets that can free you.

Break the binds.

Break the binds that hold you back,
unbind their pages
and bury them.
They don't deserve the honor of your eyes.

Break the binds that hold you dear.
Make them worn with use.
Let their words of worth be on your lips.
Break open their hope,
because in these pages,
you are unbound,
you are free.

Come and face the reflection
before you go and
look for your reflection
in the water,
and have a closer look.
Sit with the silence.
Be refreshed.
And go back out again.

2007. I was seventeen. I stood on the Alabama shoreline of West Point Lake, which straddles two states. These waves were often home to me on the Georgia shoreline, whenever I needed to wash away my spiraling thoughts. But as I now stood on the other side of the lake, the lapping water on the shore still knew how to comfort my soul.

Spring was just beginning to peek through winter's gloomy days. Foxglove flower buds were debuting fresh hues of pinks and purples, and the trees were starting to shine green again. I stood at the edge of the water pressing my feet into the sand, and as I walked, I watched all the footprints of where I'd been, knowing that I could walk for miles, and by the time I made it back around to where I'd started, the water would have washed away all memory of me. These waves had a way of cleansing. They were alive and full of possibility.

Even at this early hour, locals and college students pushed out boats and jet skis and kayaks with their paddles, eager to embrace the new season and soak in the reflection of the sun off the glistening blue. I'd never been much of a swimmer, but in that moment, I knew I needed to join them. Before I could think, I found myself knee-deep in the water, shorts and all, stepping out into the rocky region of the lake. I forgot everyone around me and focused on the cool blue current beneath me and listened to her pulse. I waded deeper and deeper into the waves, until I could no longer feel the shore beneath me at all. Suspended here, I felt free. Free to think, free to float, free to breathe.

I closed my eyes, and a thousand memories rushed over me.

I remembered the first days I came to this body of water, when I moved to campus with new hopes and a mission to leave a legacy. I remembered smells of sweat mixed with sunscreen and recalled stacks of beach towels piled high beside picnic benches while rock music blared from speakers.

I remembered all the girls with monograms and koozies mingling about aimlessly, tossing their hair and tanning their skin. I remembered how everyone clamored to be heard, rolling in and out of mindless conversations, listing their pedigrees and plans for summer vacations.

"We spent the summer in the Greek Isles."
"I hear his dad owns . . ."
"She's a legacy, isn't she?"
"All of her siblings went here . . ."

I remembered how I turned around and went back to my dorm, watching the leaves starting to fall from the trees. I remembered, from the beginning I feared this wasn't the place for me.

I opened my eyes and paddled farther, farther, farther into the lake, until the water turned glassy and still. I had never dared to come this far before. I inhaled deeply and plunged under the water to discover what lay beneath. More memories.

"You're failing," he said as he peered over his glasses to catch my eye. My professor's words assaulted my ego, and I was flooded with doubt about whether I was cut out for the rigors of academic life. I was struggling to stay afloat with the burden of all my assignments. To fail in the first semester? Fail in writing? In my mind there was no greater crime I could have committed.

"But my scholarship—" I was drowning in embarrassment, and if I didn't find my path, I would soon be drowning in financial worries as well. My throat locked up and my vision blurred. I thought of my parents, who worked long hours and poured open their wallets to supplement my studies. I promised to study harder and focus longer. But no matter how I tried, the assignments kept mounting, and I couldn't keep up. I tried to focus on my reading, but as anxiety reared its ugly head, my capacity for learning was wearing thin. I couldn't hold a single thought in my head without doubt creeping in. I couldn't learn. I knew I didn't belong there.

This memory took all my breath out of me, and I pushed back up to the lake's surface gasping for air. Failure. I was a failure.

Tears began to fall from my eyes. I looked out at the blue lake, toward the Georgia side, where I struggled so hard and yet sank so low. As far as I could see, the whole world was still and blue. No rustling in the trees and no creatures beneath me. The water was at peace.

Out of nowhere, a blackbird flew from the heights and dove low, gliding over the water back toward the Georgia side of the water. I watched her. Striking. Fierce. Free. She did not fear for tomorrow. *Why did I?*

I knew I had to face my past to move into my future. Fear had no place in these waters, and if I ever wanted to fly free, I knew it had no place in me. So I plunged under the water again and started swimming toward the Georgia shore, following the blackbird's path.

As I swam, my memories rushed back to December, when all my anxiety became unbearable and choked me off from any joy. I remembered how I approached my final exam, holding in my breath and fighting to hold back tears. I had prepared for hours and hours, but the adrenaline pulsing through me was taking over. I could hear some faint, muffled voices of the other students, but I didn't have enough energy to comprehend their words. Something about their plans with their families at Christmas and New Year's celebrations. What a luxury, to think about the future with ease and joy. All my senses tunneled to the one task at hand—passing this class—or else my future was for naught. As my professor placed the exam on my desk, my jaw locked and the words on the page shapeshifted before my eyes.

I blanked. I was empty. I had nothing left to give.

I believed my future was blank too.

I thought of all the apologies I could write or the sketches I could draw to convince my professor to give me a pass. I fidgeted at my desk and tugged on my hair. I sank deeper into my seat. My body became catatonic in defeat. I knew in that moment what was confirmed in a letter to my parents' house a few weeks later—I had failed. I failed out of college.

My parents worked so hard to provide for me, but in one crashing tidal wave, I sank all our hopes. I didn't have a category for failures who rise again, the failures who find their voices again. In movies? Sure. But in real life? No, that just didn't happen.

As the memories overtook me, I tumbled under the water, losing my sense of what was up and what was down. I swirled and flailed about, wrestling with the lies I told about myself. I had to find my way back to the top of the water. I finally opened my eyes, and I found sight of the light. I surged to the surface as water dripped from my lashes, and I fought to find sight again. I gasped for air. *Inhale, exhale,* I told myself. *Just breathe. Breathe. You are free. Your failures do not define you. They are there to teach you, not to bind you. Breathe and be free.*

I saw the blackbird soaring high in the blue sky, drifting sideways any way the wind blew. That's who I wanted to be. So fierce and so free and fearless, like her. It occurred to me, fear is conquered only when we are free to spread our wings and not hold so tightly to things. I had to let go of my manicured future and singular dreams. I had to be willing to follow the signs and look to beauty to guide me. I had to learn to trust the Light, even when I felt like I was drowning.

I paddled back to the Alabama shore, and for the first time in months, I felt like me again. Oh, it is so powerful to arise on the other side. I could not undo my story, but I could begin again.

I stepped onto the beach with new courage, unsure of what was next, but after being brought so low, I now knew that I could soar. That I was made better under those waters, and that my dreams were not finished with me yet.

Your mind floats over the trees
to where you want to be
to that wide-open space
where you feel the water's breeze,
and you struggle to manage the space between
expectation and reality.

I cannot tell you that you are free
from feeling insignificant
as you work quietly.

But I can tell you
faithfulness matters
even when progress feels small.
Your attention to this moment
is a seed being sown,
and will lead to a garden of growth.

It may take years
to see how all your hard work blooms,
but don't let the waiting
interrupt your gratitude.
You will not miss out on
what is meant for you.

WHAT WILL I
LOOK BACK ON?
WHAT WILL I
REMEMBER
OF THIS PLACE?
WHAT BEAUTIFUL TRUTHS
WILL STAY WITH ME
WHEN I AM
NO LONGER IN
AN OPEN SPACE?

I CANNOT HOLD
MY LIFE
IN THE PALM
OF MY HANDS,
BUT I CAN TRUST THAT DESPITE
WHAT I DO NOT UNDERSTAND,
I CAN TAKE THE NEXT STEPS
ON MY JOURNEY.
THE WATER WILL BE DEEPER,
BUT I WILL STAY
IN THIS DIRECTION

There are over
a hundred million lakes
on this map,
and most of them,
I will never know,
hidden in far-off places,
some open, many closed,
some carved out between pines,
others stretched long and wide.
But for every kind,
I know they all bring life—
a thousand stories
along each shore.

Water fills the lands.
I try it hold it in my hands
but I only have this map,
and I will trace and I will trace
the places I may never get to go.
All around the world
there are clearings
in the chaos
where water brings life
to us all.

I found a lake upstream
carved into the forest floor.

I dip my hands into the shallows,
fish moving out of my shadows.
I do not mean to disturb them.

So I keep a careful distance,
listen for the song of birds behind me,
watch for the flight of one before me.

I breathe deep.
I breathe deep.
This, right here, is waiting.
I'm learning to delight in my limitations
and embrace the mystery
of how I'll be remembered by history,
or if anyone will remember me at all,
or if all memory of us will pour out
like water in an overflowing lake.

Late summer rains
rush in and fill it again.
These grasses grow
higher every year,
new beginning
after new beginning.

My body softens
into the grass.
Be still, my soul,
because every day matters,
and new life will come again.

IT IS GOOD
TO HAVE LIMITS,
BUT WE
NEED TO
QUESTION:

WHO PUT
THESE LIMITS
HERE, AND
DO THEY
STAND FOR ME?

My overgrown mind clears.
I pace myself and take my time.

I will give all I have.
I will trust that there is peace.
I will lean into wisdom.
I will remember,
in the Light there is strength
to take this journey day by day,
page by page,
and trust that
I do not have to be afraid.
I am guided.
I am seen.
My story is unfolding.
I am still becoming.

COME AND BE
BY THE STREAM
MANY MILES FROM THAT OLD SEA.
SEE HOW THE LAND OPENS UP,
A WATERWAY FOR THE WEARY,
A REMINDER OF ALL THAT IS PASSING,
UNEXPLAINABLE PEACE, EVERLASTING.

LAY DOWN YOUR BURDENS
BY THE RIVERSIDE
WHERE THE WATER TRICKLES
FROM THE NORTH
INTO THE BELLY OF THE SOUTH.
IT MIGHT BE HARD
TO CATCH YOUR REFLECTION
WHEN THE WATER MOVES SO QUICKLY,
BUT THESE SHORES
CRY OUT THAT
IT MATTERS THAT
YOU ARE HERE.

YOU MADE IT THROUGH THESE TREES
AND YOU WERE MADE TO BE FREE,
AND IF NOTHING ELSE, LIVE TO SEE:
FOR ALL OF THE TROUBLE
IN YOUR SOUL,
THE RIVER
STILL FLOWS

For all the gaps in history,
the struggles you cannot fix,
the mysteries you could not solve,
the decisions that make no sense,
you will find that by grace
all along there were songs
rising up from the fields,
humming high
over the trees.

These melodies
have traveled
through the ages
to find their way to you,
singing low, singing low,
you have never been alone.
For all your soul
still longs to know,
trust these songs to carry you home.

You've arrived at this valley
where the meandering river
slopes and swings
side to side,
and must surrender to
nature's many curves.

As you walk along the riverside
notice years of agate and quartz
exposed by rushing water
crashing through the land,
through the ground.

Your mind is flooded with awe
and you want to learn the
river's wisdom
as you follow its current
wandering around the bend,
remembering the steps of
all those before you,
and all the earth that has
eroded since then.

And as you bravely
endure the course,
do not be discouraged
when much seems lost—

the land heals,
and returns to green
despite the land's unpredictability,
and you are free to breathe.

the lights dim house by house,
and I should probably go to bed,
though so much in my little mind
remains awake, unsaid.
I must accept
underneath
nighttime's faithful sky
some words will take
a thousand nights,
or maybe even a lifetime
to reach the other side
of my lips.
I must accept:
I still need rest
while I wait for ~~the~~ answers
I do not have.

For the one who came before me:

Without photographs
or birth certificates
or wedding photos
to commemorate her life,
I will hold her
in my memory.
I will make room
for her struggle,
her strength,
her story.

Perhaps this is the gift of creating,
the ability to make space
for songs unsung and memories untold.
Creating allows a new narrative to unfold:
beyond words,
beyond records,
empathy meets imagination,
looking back,
bursting into compassion,
a different kind of history—
her story.

How can I bring her with me?

D id we just cross over the river?!" I asked my mother, who had just taken over driving, as my dad took a nap in the passenger seat. The sky was oily black, only occasionally interrupted by the white lights posted alongside rest stops. Not a star hung in the sky. We had covered two time zones and changing skies and would be stopping soon for the night, but not until we made it across the river.

"We will still have about one hundred miles to go," my mother replied.

"Oh . . ." My voice drifted off as my eyes wandered to the trees, a blur of hazy green zooming behind us. I couldn't see much, but I've always felt that darkness is a prime opportunity for my imagination to light the way. My nighttime imaginary journeys, however, are always inspired by my experiences. My imagination runs parallel with reality, one under moon, one under sun, rushing like two river currents stretching toward the bay.

As a homeschool teacher, my mother leveraged every moment as a learning opportunity. Our schooling never stopped, not even in the summers. We didn't have a budget for ticketed museums and attractions, but my mother still made sure my sister and I were learning about the places we traveled. She ensured we always had access to books, and when given a choice, I would typically select the biggest book I could find—usually a volume of the encyclopedia on one of the top shelves in our home's library. Their crimson-red cloth and embossed gold-lettering enticed me, and I loved feeling like I could conquer the hardest books on the shelves like a true academic. I'd stand on my tiptoes, outstretch my fingers, and jump to grab whatever book I could reach.

One day I came crashing down into my chair under the weight of the letter *M*. I quickly found my bearings and then carefully flipped through each page, stopping on words that felt familiar in some way. *Maps, Mississippi (History of), Music, Mystery* . . . I knew I'd seen Mississippi before on our road-trip map! I turned to that entry and examined the old photos before me. One was from 1860. A map of Issaquena County, featuring a river and plantations, with little squares on each property to indicate slave quarters.

I didn't understand every word, but I understood the general context and let my imagination fill in the gaps. I flipped through the full-color photographs and oil paintings of governors and generals, whose faces were stern as they sat posing for their portraits. I could feel the determination of their eyes piercing through the page. I wondered when they became so hardened and what they were like when they were young, like me. I fixed my gaze farther down the page to discover a much smaller photo, in black and white. The photograph seemed to have been taken in a flash, for all of the faces were blurry and hard to make out. All I could see were shadows of figures standing in front of a one-room house. I was drawn to one of an unnamed girl with tightly coiled hair, tucked in plaits behind her ears, which was how I used to wear my hair.

And now, as we were driving in the middle of the night, her face flashed across my mind's eye once again. I looked out my window to see these trees, which have stood here for ages and may hold the truth about her journey. Our stories were buried in their trunks, and they could whisper horrors unspeakable, if asked. I strained my eyes to try to make out their colors, shapes, and textures, to see if they would tell me what they knew. But no matter how hard I looked, I saw only layers of darkness. Perhaps I needed to listen. I asked my mother if I could roll down the window, despite the wind and the rain, and she allowed me. A sliver of hot air instantly lapped against the window, and then another. It was a stormy, humid night, and the heat swept through the cracked window in waves, pulsing and whirring like the rhythm of a drum. I heard a branch snap.

I imagined the girl and her mother, running in step with the drumming wind, and with every step, they knew the sound of the smallest branch snapping beneath their feet could condemn them. Even the trees could not be trusted.

I shuddered to think of the children who looked like me who didn't have this luxury of mobility. To travel freely, crossing borders, one state to the next. Oh, but why should it be a luxury? To walk? To run?

When I asked my mother about when we'd reach the Mississippi River, she was able to calculate how many miles we had to go. But for that young girl, when she asked her mother for directions, it's likely her mother did not know. Her mother probably whispered sweet lies of comfort as they traveled deep into the night, which would have been the kindest option available in those conditions. She would have led them west, with the hope of swimming toward freedom. These trees were their only shields, and time was a precious commodity.

Meanwhile, my mother steered us swiftly through the woods, while my sister slept peacefully. Mom's feet never even touched the earth. We drove like any other day, soaring across a hundred miles, within the safety of the car's armor and might. But the girl and her mother on the other side of the trees were trudging through mud, twisting their ankles in the earth and skirting over broken tree limbs. I imagined myself reaching across the trees toward them, offering them an escape in our car, but I was too late. I was aching to travel back in time to them and carry them into their future freedom.

I want to write stories to change her history. What stories might she have written had she been allowed to write? What discoveries might she have made if her travels were not solely an escape at night? I think of the unmarked white pages of the journal she might have, and the black ink that she would put on that page with eloquence and grace. Maybe she would build her own encyclopedia of stories worthy of beautiful black binding. I will never know who she really was, but I believe in her power to speak.

A lot can happen in a hundred miles or a hundred years, but I do not believe we've come far enough.

As we approached the Mississippi, I saw the bridge illuminated by the highway lights, harsh and encroaching on my mind's eye. I was immediately jolted back to the present. I wasn't quite ready for that kind of light. I wasn't ready to leave her behind. As we approached the bridge, the lights grew wider and I fought harder to hold on to the thought of that woman and her daughter. What if they don't know how to swim? How deep is the water? How will they make it through?

I held my breath and closed my eyes and braced myself for the long journey over the bridge to Louisiana. As my mom steered us toward the bridge, she quietly pulled to the side of the road. She woke my dad.

"Sorry, I just don't like driving over these bridges," she said to him.

My parents switched seats, he put the engine in drive, and we rolled across the lower Mississippi River. I peered down into the dark water. I remembered from my reading that the river was used as a passageway for steamboats for many years, and I expected it to be dense with coagulated grease and fuel. However, even beneath the hovering white lights on the bridge, the skin on the water looked like a piece of black velvet, smooth and luxurious.

I knew I had a choice to look at that water with care to see its protecting waves that brought so many people into freedom. Even without specific knowledge of the Black girls whose stories were never recorded, when I listened to that beautiful black water, I could hear its mysteries. I looked through the window, and I took a picture with my mind. Surely, surely, surely they made it across. I chose freedom for her. I needed to.

With only a few more seconds until we reached the other side of the bridge, the lights finally faded away. I turned back for one last glance to see the road narrowing behind us through the trees outstretched for miles and miles. They seemed a little taller now. They stood there speechless, holding on to their secrets.

The waters were quiet then, and we continued on, westward, to start another day.

I CANNOT PREDICT WHAT'S NEXT,
BUT I CAN CHOOSE HOW I RESPOND
IN THE WAY I CROSS THESE WATERS,
AND THE WAY THAT I LOVE,
IN THE WAY I REMEMBER TRUTH
AND LET IT INFUSE WHO I BECOME

DESPITE THE CHAINS THAT HELD YOU BACK,
YOUR HEARTBEAT IS EVIDENCE
THAT EVEN HERE, HOPE CAN LAST.

AS YOU TRAVEL ALONG THE PATH,
GRASPING AT BLACK SCALES OF
BARK FLAKING OFF THESE TREES,
MAY THIS DARKNESS REMIND YOU
FAITH GOES BEYOND
WHAT IS SEEN.

LOVE IS GREATER THAN FEAR,

AND YOU ARE FREE TO BE ALIVE HERE.

How beautifully
you absorb Light
in the layers of your skin,
luminous as ink
lifting off the page.
Even when no words are spoken,
you still find songs to hum along
with music notes sung in color
to create a song,
"I am whole,
beautiful,
free."

I HAVE KNOWN THE FOREST,
THE FLOODPLAINS,
AND THE RIVER THAT
 SLIPS DOWN INTO THE SEA.
I HAVE KNOWN SLEEPLESS NIGHTS
I WAS CERTAIN WOULD BREAK ME—

AND I HAVE ALSO KNOWN
THE SOUND OF
FREEDOM CALLING,
AND THE BEAT OF THE DRUM OF
MY HEART.
I HAVE KNOWN
DESPITE WHAT I WAS TOLD,
I AM WORTHY OF A BRAND-NEW START.

☐ laundry to fold.
☐ photographs to take.
☐ memories to make
   in thankless tasks
   on ordinary days

I long to go
   I long to stay

YOU WILL CROSS RELENTLESS OCEANS
YOU WISH WOULD RISE AND SPLIT IN
TWO. YOU WILL MEET PEOPLE WHO
BELIEVE IN A HELPING HAND, AND
YOU WILL MEET OTHERS WHOSE FEAR
HOLDS THEM BACK FROM TRYING TO
UNDERSTAND. YOU WILL FIND A SENSE
OF PEACE WHERE THE LOW RIVER BENDS,
AND YOU WILL RUN BENEATH A CANOPY
OF MIDNIGHT TREES, WONDERING
WHEN THEY WILL END. YOU WILL
TRAVEL NORTH, WONDERING IF
YOU ARE ENOUGH, AND YOU WILL
NEVER OUTRUN THE FLOW OF
ENDLESS, BOUNDLESS LOVE.

MAY WE SHARE IN
OUR SUFFERING.
MAY WE SHARE IN
OUR TRIUMPHS
AND THE DIFFICULT CHAPTERS.
MAY WE SHARE IN OUR JOY.
MAY WE SHARE IN OUR GRIEF.
MAY WE SHARE IN
TRUSTING LOVE
THAT GOES BEYOND
WHAT WE SEE.

The moon pierces through
the yellow-green leaves
draped like strips of fine linen
to illuminate the black limbs of the willow,
who stretches her arms into the sky
in majesty
rising to the occasion of Night,
and her dancing leaves whisper truths that
all that is wrong will be made right.

Keep breathing.
Keep breathing
Absorb the air around you
like a tree
rooted by the riverbank
unafraid of the heat
leaves green
free
to just be
present
with no need
to solve anything.

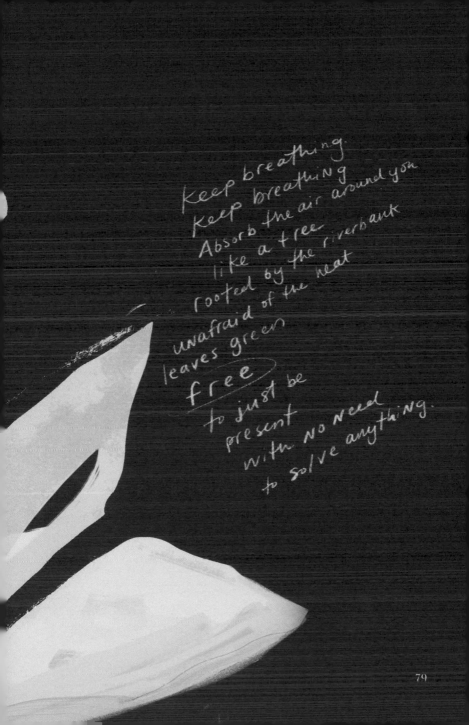

When all of this is over,
I'll take shelter under the orange tree
that sits in the shadow of the old oak tree
cloaked under the sky, wide and black.

I can trust and believe,
despite the sorrow stored in my skin,
joy is a steady stream
in the depths of my soul,
and the midnight sky a balm
for my sundried arms.

I am not who I was,
I do not have to run anymore.
I have hope,
this day is still brimming with a thousand stories.

And my story is one of many.

Under the orange tree,
under the oak tree,
my words
unassembled
within me,
I peel back this orange
layer by layer
to tell its story.
And then I peel another one,
and another.
I taste their sweet and sour cacophonies,
each piece of fruit in its own season.

Leaning against the brown tree trunk,
I weep,
finally.
Under all these shredded layers,
I am finally
free to rest.

Just below
the trunk of the tree
you will find roots widespread,
creating a structure,
a network
of life
and hope.
After all we endured
we have grown strong,
limbs stretched wide,
doing good,
faithful work.
The roots of the tree
holding
how we have survived,
the fruit of the tree
showing
how we have thrived.
May we never forget the growth
that has happened underground.
May we never forget the strength
and courage
we have found.

FILL THE MARGINS OF YOUR LIFE
WITH YOUR OWN ADDITIONS.
LET YOUR OWN STORIES BE
ROOTED AND GROUNDED AT THE CENTER,
EVEN IF YOU ARE THE ONLY ONE
WHO EVER SEES THE ENDING.

WHAT MATTERS IS THAT YOU ARE TRUSTING
THAT YOU DO NOT NEED PERMISSION
TO WRITE YOUR NARRATIVE
AND HAVE YOUR SAY.

IT MATTERS HOW YOU TELL THE STORY.
NO ONE ELSE TELLS IT THAT WAY.

Pink blooms in spring,
a cardinal's red wings,
the fresh grass after the rain.

You have endured pain,
but have courage to see color.

You have wrestled with questions
that no one else seems to understand.
Weathering storms that were never
to make it to your land.
You have wondered why
these troubles did not stay at sea.

Heavy gray skies press down upon you,
but you choose to delight
in life
one breath at a time,
pursuing peace,
holding on to truth,
so rest
and let healing
find you.

HAVE COURAGE, HEAVY HEART. FIND JOY IN THE IN-BETWEEN.

87

When she looked back at those old photographs,
she was shocked by
the sadness on her face.
Even though she stands shoulder-to-shoulder
in packs of people,
she feels worlds away.

The words in that girl's heart
are sobering and clear.
She still feels tightness in her chest
even though it's been thirteen years.

Am I too much? Not enough?

Yet today, she can laugh
because now she knows
from the phone conversation only an hour ago,
she is not alone anymore,
and even though she and her new friends
do not live door-to-door,
they feel closer than ever before.

She still grieves what she lost,
but she is grateful for who she has come to know.
She is learning to trust she is worthy
of love, of being seen and known.

IT TAKES
BRAVERY
TO CONNECT.
WE'RE ALL WORTHY
OF LOVE AND GRACE.

NO MATTER WHERE YOU
FIND YOURSELF IN THIS
LANDSCAPE,

NEVER FORGET
WHO YOU ARE
AND ALL THE GOOD
YOU CAN DO,
SHOWING UP WITH
LOVE AND OPEN HANDS,
AND EVEN WITHOUT WORDS,
SAYING, "I SEE YOU."

THIS IS ABUNDANCE
OVER SCARCITY:
EVEN WHEN YOU DO NOT
FEEL LIKE YOU HAVE MUCH,
YOU CAN STILL SHOW UP
WITH LOVE.

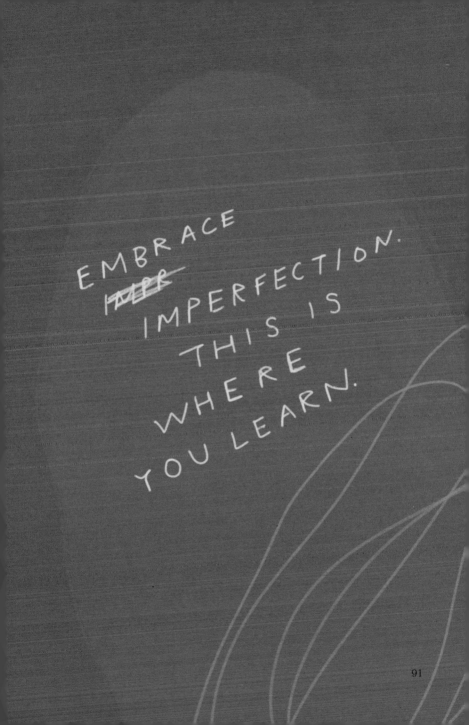

EMBRACE
~~IMPE~~
IMPERFECTION.
THIS IS
WHERE
YOU LEARN.

When spring comes
and the sky is still overcast with gray,
and your throat is dry, and there is no rain.
Only dust and dirt and work.
More work.
Not enough hands.
Not enough help.
You need help.

Breathe deep,
breathe deep.
You are still loved,
and you are seen
even though your mind is prone to think
this place you loved is better off without you.

It takes courage to stay
and fight for play.
But there will be a day
when we will laugh again.

You drift out from the shore.
You have never been this far away before.

You ebb and flow through worry,
through waves of insecurity,
trying to stay strong
in the flood.
Restless, anxious thoughts
clog your ears,
cloud your vision.

Your feet can't find the ground.
Which way is the sky? Which way is down?

You long for an embrace,
bending down,
bringing you up to the light of day,
whispering,
gently,
"You'll be okay."
But those arms have not yet come,
and you remain undone.
How do I go forward on this day?
Oh, dear soul, please wait.
Wait again, like watchmen wait for morning.

PURPLE SKIES TONIGHT.
SPECKS OF LIGHT.
IN FAR-AWAY WINDOWS,
SHADOWED HANDS,
CLANKING GLASSES,
CLEARING DISHES.
YOUR TIRED HEART
   STARTS TO WONDER
WILL I EVER FIND MY PLACE?

THROUGH THE WASHING
WAVES OF DISCONNECTION,
YOU HAVE MANAGED
TO BE STRONG,
YOU HAVE MANAGED TO STAY.

GRACE.

MORNING IS COMING,
OF THIS YOU CAN BE SURE.
INVITE TODAY IN
AND LOOK TO SEE
ANOTHER WANDERING SOUL
WHO IS FEELING
THE SAME WAY

Three years after Hurricane Katrina devastated New Orleans, the city was still reeling without support. A conglomerate of local organizations from surrounding colleges, churches, and community groups organized a service trip to help rebuild homes, businesses, and even a local playground in the city.

When I first learned about the opportunity to serve, I immediately signed up, along with a group of girls from my dormitory. Even though we moved in at the same time, they all seemed as if they already knew each other. Most people in my dorm were athletes with busy schedules, so it was difficult to find the time to make friends with them. But these girls, like me, were not involved in any organized sports, and I was eager to get to know them. I could hear their laughter through the walls of my dorm room, giving minute-by-minute commentary on Matthew McConaughey's southern drawl, sometimes all night long. They seemed inseparable, and since my own roommate was an athlete who was often at practice or out of town playing away games, I so deeply wanted to experience that kind of bond.

As a homeschooled kid, it seemed like no matter how I tried, I still found myself on the outside. But lo and behold, one day I found myself sitting beside two of the girls in a history class, wearing comfy hoodies and loose ponytails just like me, and they slowly became my first two friends in college.

The word *friend* is debatable. We'd linger in the hallway between our rooms and share notes before a big test. This wasn't the experience I'd dreamed of, but slowly but surely, I felt they were letting me in their circle. I knew this trip to New Orleans was the first big test of our friendship.

Our trip was scheduled over Easter weekend, and it was the

first time any of us had spent the holiday away from our families. It was strange to be away from family, but I felt a duty to these new friendships that had bloomed over the course of the semester. Here we were, venturing out into the unknown together, to help others in need.

One by one, all the volunteers filed out of our dorm and onto the bus that would take us to New Orleans. With my bag on my back and sleeping bag tucked under my arm, I followed my friends onto a crowded bus filled with students from other colleges. "On the Road Again" blasted from the speaker while an upperclassmen in a T-shirt and sunglasses cheered us on to get ready for a life-changing weekend. We found our way to the back where I soon discovered the seats were in twos. I looked on as the four girls quickly paired off, and it became clear I'd be alone for the seven-hour drive. I immediately felt my insecurities resurfacing. One more day sitting on the outside.

This trip predated smartphones, and I didn't have room in my bag for books, so I was left alone with my thoughts. Time seemed to slow down as I looked back at my group of friends getting situated in their seats for the long ride. They pulled out a deck of cards, their familiar laughter erupting within minutes. We hadn't even made it to the interstate, but I could feel myself teeming with jealousy. Only a few rows of colorful carpeted seats separated us, but the aisle felt like it stretched for miles. My eyes fixated on their reflections in the window, although I'm not sure what I was hoping to see. I overheard traces of their conversations, and my lonely heart flooded with sadness.

We arrived in New Orleans late in the night. As the counselors imparted basic instructions for lodging, I snuck glances toward my friends, who were helping one another carry their bags and blankets to their bunks. I had no plans to reunite with them at that moment, and I was primarily frustrated with myself for not managing my feelings better. Wasn't I used to this by now? Living my life on the outer rings?

We filed into a large, open hall in the building where we would be sleeping that night. Feeling sluggish from the trip, I knew I had to get some rest. We had a long weekend ahead of us, and I came here to do good work. *This isn't about me,* I reminded myself. I laid down in my sleeping bag beside some girls I had never met, but I didn't bother to make conversation. I turned my back as their chatter reverberated around the room. I burrowed deeper in my little black hole of blue polyester, closed my eyes, and let out a deep breath before drifting off to sleep thinking about the playground we were going to be building tomorrow. I imagined myself being six years old again, my eyes lighting up at the sight of newly built monkey bars to conquer. That would have meant the world to me.

I woke up in the morning ready to work. Working with my hands has always made me feel closer to God. Whether stroking paint onto the page or tapping a hammer's head to a nail or securing a seed in the dirt, I know I'm at my best when my hands are active. These hands are agents of love, and in that moment, I needed to find something to love.

We approached a new set of buses, which had separate destinations all around the city. I hung back for a moment, deciding whether to reconcile with my friends or not. In a split-second decision, I decided to venture out on my own. I needed to focus on the task at hand, and I hoped, perhaps, the work could bring me joy.

As we rolled into the city of Katrina, I was overwhelmed by the devastation. It was like a war zone. It broke my heart to see dilapidated schools and drowned-out cemeteries, still unsettled three years later. In the muggy air, my nostrils flared at the smell of acrid saltiness washed up into homes. Mold coagulated on the walls, and I could feel my mind growing foggy. The locals were assured that all their devastation would be healed by time, but I had eyes. I saw their lives in the rubble. I smelled the smells. Who would stand with them? Who cared about them? The pretense of caring made me speechless—even more than the hurricane itself. It felt so unfair.

As we pulled up to a destroyed community gym, I was overwhelmed by the amount of work to be done, even three years later. I felt guilty. *Why didn't I come to help sooner? Why hadn't I done more?* Sure, I was a college freshman without many resources of my own. And yet I had more than the twelve-year-old boy I saw walking in the rain beside the empty lots of trash piles and bricks. I felt an obligation to him. I needed to help him.

That's our duty, right? To care until it hurts? To look to the hills where our help comes from, with open arms, ready to extend the love we have been given? I was shocked by my inability to practice boundless love.

I filed off the bus. A heavy breeze tunneled down the street and caught me off guard by its sharp coldness. I shoved my hands into my pockets and clenched them into fists. We stood on the backside of a gym that had been hollowed out by the hurricane. Some of the structure was still intact, but the smell of damp wood made me question how much longer it could keep standing. *Were we too late?*

A worker for the local organization facilitating this project assigned tasks and began to pass out brooms to sweep the floorboards. As we worked, the Gulf wind whipped through the gaping holes in the walls, making our attempt to clean feel futile.

How do you repair an entire ecosystem, when every part of the whole depends on the other? Nonetheless, I carried on the best I could beside my colleagues, never learning their names, pressed back by the winds, often blown into one another. I wondered how heavy the wind must have felt on that devastating day three years previous. I wondered if the people seeking shelter in this gym knew one another's names.

After lunch, our nameless crew departed for another dilapidated gym. It looked awfully similar to the one we had just left, only this time there were traces of posters left on the wall. I traced my hand over one small corner of bright purple still there. I saw a little speck of yellow and green. The brush strokes  on the wall appeared to be painted by children. My heart sunk. Where did they go after the storm? I looked around at the rest of the crew as we swept the room in silence again.

I imagined this trip filled with joyous interaction. I thought I would be working alongside a group of other young women whom I naively believed would be my forever-friends. I imagined reconvening with them ten years from then, reflecting on stories of how we worked together on this trip. We would rehash inside jokes. We would talk about how meaningful it was to gather on Easter, on a playground, where children greeted us with laughter. At this point, my vision for the weekend was completely washed away. I planned for community and gathering and conversation, but I was met with silence. And in silence, I let my thoughts drift to crumbled drywall and dirt in dustpans.

After another long night's sleep, I awoke to head out to our last stop on the trip—yet another gym—for an Easter service. Unfortunately, my bus arrived a little late, and I missed a good portion of it, which was a new experience. As a preacher's kid, I had never missed an Easter service in my life. Like many others, I was used to a traditional church setting on this day, but without the comforts of my home church or friends, I was particularly struck by the message of the day—that hope was alive even within these battered walls and dust. Hope is present in all of us, even in the worst of conditions, and even when we're all alone.

As the service ended, the trip organizers made an announcement. We were making one last stop at the playground before heading back to campus. The sky was overcast and gray, but I was overcome with warmth as children and their families from around the neighborhood filled the park. I stood as a bystander on the edge of the playground. A sense of stillness washed over me as I watched parents walk up to the park holding the hands of their children, slowly letting go to watch their kids run free and explore.

I glanced over to see the girls I originally came with, but I never approached them. The Gulf's sea-salt air and devastated earth were stirring something new in me, and I found myself at peace in the dissonance. My heart was softening. Sometimes acts of service are best done in silence. Sometimes you end up pushing a broom by yourself, and that's exactly where you are supposed to be. When my heart shifted and I worked without expectation, I found myself happiest of all. When we live with care for our neighbors, we find life. A sea-change indeed.

We piled back onto the bus. My shoulders finally gave way, after days of work for both my mind and body. I walked by my dorm-mates, who had found a new set of seats toward the front of the bus. We shared a quick laugh about how we had papers due in the morning, and we were so glad we had finished them before the trip because we were exhausted now. On my way to find a seat, I recognized two girls who had been at the gyms yesterday. I sat down beside them and asked their names, and as the bus rolled onto the interstate, we reminisced on our shared experience as we settled into the rhythm of the road.

Many of the questions I asked in my hours of sweeping in New Orleans went unanswered. The devastation took hundreds of lives and displaced a million people. My broom and dustpan couldn't fix that. My anger and frustration were unabated. And even though my heavy heart wanted to fix everything, I had to let that be. The story of neglect could not be unwritten, and I wrestled with not knowing whether our efforts were actually making a difference. I concluded that we can't wait for perfect answers before we start doing good available to us. We have a choice to be present. We have a choice to write new endings, even for storylines we didn't start. We don't need to be powerful insiders before we show up for others living on the outside. We can serve, and maybe no one will notice, but we can still act in love. In fact, we must. And when we do, we are made new.

> How far am I from New Orleans now?
> Not far at all.
> I will always remember that place.
> A place of silent service,
> reverence,
> ready to give of myself
> without needing to say a word.

AS I STAND IN THE
EMPTY CRESCENT
WHERE THE WATER USED TO BE,
FIGHTING TO REMEMBER
HOW TO LIVE PURPOSEFULLY
AMIDST WHAT'S MISSING
MAYBE I WILL FIND IN THE GULF
ROOM TO HEAR
ALL THE MORE CLOSELY
THE RHYTHM OF
MY OWN HEARTBEAT.

I AM NOT ALONE
WHEN I'M ALONE.
I HAVE NOT
MISSED OUT ON
WHAT WAS
MEANT FOR ME

AND MAYBE,
AFTER ALL THAT WE LOST
AND ALL THAT WE ARE
STILL GRIEVING,
WE CAN BEGIN TO SEE
THERE IS NO CLEAR DIVIDE
BETWEEN YOU AND ME,
AND EVEN WITHOUT SPEAKING,
WE CAN GROW IN
GENTLENESS,
RESPECT.
WE WERE MADE
FOR COMMUNITY,
DESIGNED
TO CONNECT.

Light always casts shadow.
Storm clouds find us on sunny days.
But realize this means that
the Swamp Sunflowers
with their bright yellow arms
stretching up from the low, wet grass,
just might keep blooming okay.

Death becomes life where
we thought the road would end.
Hope rises out of nothing and
we realize Light pours in.
Our hope is radiant.
We get to join in on the dance,
over and over again,
as long as we live,
we receive Love,
and we bring it in,
and we give and we give and we give.

Love goes beyond language.
Love interrupts thoughts
and is boundless in her might.

Let love meet you in your hiding place.
Let love meet you in the mystery.

Divine
yes, Divine
meets you
right here where you are,
not just your tomorrow self.
Oh no, you are loved today.

SILVER STRINGS PULLED TIGHT
ACROSS THE HOLLOW BODY OF WOOD.
PRESSED AND PULLED
SHE SINGS
IN THE TENSION

BEAUTY IS MADE
POSSIBLE.

AND TOGETHER,
WE BRING OUR STRINGS
TAUT, WORN AND OUT OF TUNE,
TO CREATE A SYMPHONY.

FEEL VIBRATIONS
FROM THE SOUNDS,
AND DELIGHT
IN THE RESTS.

ALLOW TIME
TO FEEL
IN BETWEEN
the
HARMONIES.

For all that is lost and still not recovered,
allow your hope to bound forward
in the abandoned streets
where others' hopes used to be.

May you lead the way from the water that destroyed
to a water that brings life.
Let your passions turn into compassion.
Make beautiful things that speak to the value
of those around you.

Give time. Give space. Give smiles and give your peace,
and perhaps, it can never be said enough:
give grace.
Just be.
Maybe you feel unqualified
and you do not know why.

Think of the Kallima butterfly
folding her wings to resemble a leaf.
She is muted, and she is beautiful and purposed all the same
even when others do not see.
She does not make herself known in the way other butterflies do,
but she still shows up exactly how she was meant to.

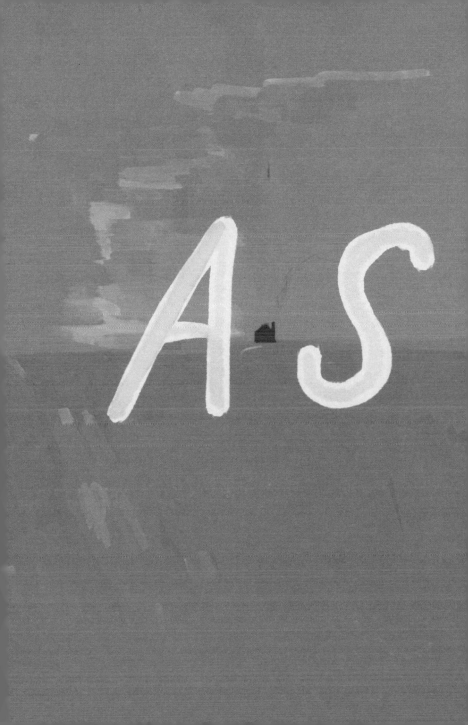

Morning, still rising,
has left a fog
on my window.
I wait until
my gaze
comes to know
the honey-speckled
green leaves
slowly dancing
in the dawn
right in front of me.

I am grateful they have
nowhere else to be.

THERE
ARE MORE
IDEAS
UP AHEAD
OF ME

OCHRE CLOUDS
FILL THE SKY.
THE SUN IS LOW,
MY HOPES
ARE HIGH.
I DO NOT
ALWAYS STOP
AND NOTICE LIGHT,
BUT I WILL
CONTINUE
TO TRY

There will be seasons of life
where the work you have done
will feel like it is not enough.
You will feel like you've reached the height
of what you can do.
A voice whispers over the fields
telling you to rest.
Wake up.
Eat.
Take another step.
Come and find peace.

Yellow stalks turn gold under the right light.
Not at all hours—
only twice a day.

Trust in the rhythms of this moment,
knowing you will glow again.

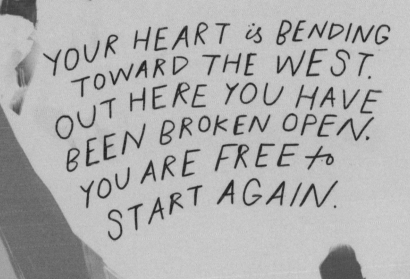

YOUR HEART is BENDING TOWARD THE WEST. OUT HERE YOU HAVE BEEN BROKEN OPEN. YOU ARE FREE to START AGAIN.

THE WIND,
THE RAIN, AND
THE SUN
COMBINE
TO MAKE
A LIFE.

WHAT A
miracle
IT IS
TO WAKE
EVERY DAY.

Beneath this
silhouette of power lines,
a thousand miles away
from ponderosa pines,
I paint a watercolor sky
in my mind.
Rain bellows outside
in bass notes,
and I feel a melody
rising up inside me.

I do not know
what lies ahead,
but here in the open
I am free.

For most of our marriage, my husband, Patrick, and I moved all over the map, attempting to make our livelihood in the music industry. We had youthful grit, and we were determined to make it.

But sometimes, no matter how much you prepare, the journey to your dreams can wear you down. Rejection was constant, and bills were mounting. It seemed as soon as we made it through one valley, another would present itself.

We worked hard, we played hard, and we loved our craft. But we were sinking financially, and our lifestyle on the road started to take an emotional toll. We moved all around Atlanta and Nashville, lugging boxes from one apartment to another, trying to find our place in the thriving music scenes.

The rhythms of this unrooted lifestyle were beginning to drain my creativity. I was becoming a version of myself I didn't enjoy, and playing music began to feel foreign to me, as if someone else was singing when I opened my mouth. I was losing a bit of myself at every tour stop, but we didn't have the luxury of slowing down and considering how to improve our lives. We were rolling full steam ahead, and we couldn't find the brakes.

Under the pressure of the industry and of our bank account, I knew we needed something new, but in this valley of life, I couldn't see a path forward. We needed to find somewhere safe and open to clear our heads. Somewhere we would feel free from comparison and free from seven-dollar lattes.

One summer day, in the midst of a national tour, my husband and I had a few hours to spare at our hotel just outside of Dallas, Texas. Like any tired, broke couple, we decided it was in our best interest to order pizza and turn in early. As we leaned against the tour bus waiting for the pizza guy, we were struck by how the land folded open in every direction. I was amazed at how far the blue skies stretched on.

I was alert for the first time in weeks, maybe months. It was quiet, solemn, serene.

"Are you seeing this, Patrick?"

I could see all around me, for miles. The sun was beginning to set, and a watercolor pool of pinks and purples took over, creating a cotton-candy backdrop for a silhouetted cityscape. After months of exhaustion and disconnection, I finally felt alive to myself once again. Lyrics roared inside of me, and I felt that spark to create.

Patrick gave me a knowing glance, and while we stood outside under the pink sky, we began to discuss the possibility of starting anew in this land. Dallas was the solution we were craving. These open plains promised us freedom and possibility, and the idea of making this our home took root in our hearts.

As the colors began to fade from the sky, we tipped our delivery driver, grabbed our pizza, headed indoors, and huddled up together on the edge of our hotel bed to plan our future life here. Before I could even finish my garlic knots, we realized this dream could soon be our reality. No more cramped apartments we couldn't afford. No more living paycheck to paycheck. No more pressure to dress a certain way or attend the right parties or know the right people. I started to dream of office nooks and bookshelves and a washing machine. Yes, a washing machine. *Farewell, nomad life.* We were here to stay.

We completed the tour, and with only a few dollars to our name, we returned to Nashville, packed whatever we could fit into our car and headed west. Every bump in the road felt like one hop over a front-porch floorboard, like the ones I counted on the porch that day in 1996 on the porch getting ready for the first big road trip of my life.

But as beautiful as Dallas proved to be, it did not erase the problems we were running from. Our finances were still in disarray, and that spark I felt that day in the parking lot quickly started to diminish. There were bills to pay, and there were still gigs far away to play too. I found myself rushing up and down the highway, in and out of the Dallas Love Field airport, trying to keep afloat long enough so that this newfound Texas dream could take off.

One November night, all of life's struggles started to feel unbearable. Rain battered the house all day, and the humidity hung on the porch and seeped beneath the cracks of the door. Even the carpet felt moist as I tucked my bare feet beneath me where I sat at my computer, desperately searching for any spark of inspiration for my next step as a musician. In the journal open before me, I scribbled down a list of buzzwords like *marketing plan* and *business statement*, hoping for an epiphany of how to make some money. But as I sat there trying to forge a new plan for my life, nothing came. I started to doubt if I was ever meant to come to this place.

Each drop of rain seemed to echo in my ears. Still, the voices in my mind raged louder. Every single voice that had told me I was never good enough settled deep in my mind, their lies piling up like stones forged in the earth. I came here for clear skies and clarity, but now, in the darkness and never-ending rain, I couldn't see my path forward as an artist.

The rain outside turned into hail, beating on the roof. I stuffed my journal into a drawer, only to find a stack of unpaid bills. Tears welled in my eyes and splattered onto my desk. Maybe the dream of making art was over for me long ago, and I was the last one to know.

Lightning struck.

I was done. I grabbed my journal out of the drawer and flipped to a new page, resolved to write my last song. This was it. It was time to grow up and leave art behind for a path that would provide. No more storytelling.

I was incapable of finding a melody. So instead of a song, I let the words rain down in poetry.

> When you start to feel
> like things should have been better this year
> remember the mountains and valleys
> that brought you here.
> They were not mistakes
> and those moments were not in vain.
> You are not the same.

You have grown and you are growing.
You are living, you are breathing.
You are wrapped in endless, boundless grace.
And things will get better.
There is more to you than yesterday.

I read the words back to myself:

remember the mountains and valleys
that brought you here . . .

The mountains and valleys I trekked all over this country brought me here to these open plains of Dallas. And in this place laid bare, I was even more aware of every failure. I could not escape myself. I couldn't escape my flaws. There were no stories I could tell to undo the fact that I couldn't pay my bills and never heard my songs on the radio. I failed, plain and simple. *There is more to you than yesterday . . .*

I shook my head in disbelief. I did not believe my own words. Maybe someday in the future they would ring true. But today? Today I was just as unsuccessful as yesterday, and I had a hunch that tomorrow I would be too.

The thunder roared once more, and I was done. I took a picture of the poem, closed my journal, and then, as a proud millennial, I posted it in a corner of the internet that I was certain no one would see. An ode to failure. An ode to the artist in me. Farewell, music and poetry.

That night I started brainstorming new career paths with salaries. Maybe I would go back to school and get an MBA. It was time to build a real résumé. It was time for more respectable, impressive work.

No more heading further west.
No more chasing sunsets.
It was time to grow up.

Two months later, with MBA applications cluttering my desktop, surrounded by cover letters for jobs I didn't want, I logged online only to find a message from a stranger who said she had seen something I wrote. She sent me the photograph of my farewell poem, scratched in pencil on my journal, marked with tears and insecurity. She said it gave her hope. It struck my heart to know my hard moment could be of use to another woman.

In the weeks to come, I was flooded with messages of friends and strangers who found my words, and to this day, I do not know how it found its way into the crevices and corners of the internet. But in time, I learned my words penned in desperation were ushering in hope to hundreds of thousands of people.

And finally, I let those words of hope seep into my heart too.

I opened the journal again back to where I had written the poem. I looked at all the white space surrounding it. I counted the twelve lines I had written, my honest thoughts simply scripted on the page. Twelve simple lines, written in fury and shared in strength.

I can never repay these dear open plains of Texas. I trusted this place to expose me for who I was—my beauty and my flaws in equal measure, and sure enough, they did. I wanted to see myself plainly, and Dallas offered me the freedom to explore who I was meant to be. In these flat, airy plains, I couldn't tell myself any more lies. Just as I could see the full spectrum of the sunset, I learned to see the full spectrum of me. My hopes and my dreams, my failures and inconsistencies. The rain came, and it was hard, and the rain left, and sure enough, clear blue skies always came again.

As the messages from new followers flooded in, I penned my responses to these strangers—as many as I could. They saw something in my words that I hadn't seen myself, and that is the power of language.

I stack words until they become lines, and lines into poems, poems into power—the power to hope again. Lena from Phoenix, Imani from Philadelphia, and Taylor from Miami—their names and stories have survived in my memory, and I write for them. I write to connect, because I know in my core, we are all more alike than we are different. I write in honesty and imperfection, knowing things will get better, and together, we have a gift of grace. So no matter the stage of life—whether in open plains, valleys, or mountains—I believe we have a duty to connect, a duty to share, a duty to create in our calling, whatever that may be.

Come back down
to the beat of your heart.
Come back to the joy of color.
Come back home to believing
hope still runs in your veins.

You're finding your way
in the wind,
but you can always come
back to Light again.

We dreamers
have a duty
to carry on.

We leave so much behind,
untangling old desires one at a time,
never knowing which parts of them
will make it above the rooflines.
And yet still, we trust,
there will be more to see.
What matters is that
we believed every word, and then
we let them go.
We let them breathe.

THE MOON
BEARS
BOTH SHADOWS
AND LIGHT.

ON THIS COLD,
SHARP NIGHT,

REMIND YOURSELF
IT IS ALRIGHT.
REMIND YOURSELF
IT IS ALRIGHT

TO BE MORE
TO FEEL ALIVE.

AND THEN,
FALL ASLEEP
JUST FINE.

THE STORY
YOU SHARED
MADE
ONE VOICE
FEEL HEARD

TOMORROW
WILL BE GRAND.
SLOW DOWN
TAKE REST.
BEFORE YOU
BEGIN AGAIN

Down in the desert plain
deep in the night,
the moon arrives,

filling summer's evening sky.
There, on the ground
where dust wisps around your feet,
you notice sharp, brawny leaves.
Now fully blooming,

the yucca flower
painting herself white,
flickering outward and upward,
nature's candlelight.

Lamparas de Dios—
Lamps of God,
some say—
for during the day,
she tucks her petals
to hide from the heat,
but under evening's brow,

she sighs and peeks out,

tender
and free
to shine ever-so brightly
when you thought she'd be asleep.

Come alive, come alive,
deep into the night,
come and dance and wave and stretch

under the moon's loving gaze.

TASTE THE GIFT
OF THE DIVINE
AS DUST BLOWS BY,
a praise
FOREVER ON YOUR LIPS.
YOU STRUGGLE
TO SPEAK OF IT
AS YOU REMEMBER
THE WORLD IS MADE
FROM SPECKS THAT ARE SMALL,

AND SOMEHOW, GRACIOUSLY,
YOU ARE PART OF IT ALL.

in uncharted land,
  you have no choice
    but to look up.
      lost under the stars—

  is there anything better?

  and when the sun
    peeks through again,
      you'll know that life
        is a miracle

BE SPEECHLESS.
ASK WHY.
ENGAGE IN MYSTERY
FOR THE REST OF
YOUR LIFE.

THIS IS FAITH—
LETTING GO OF
NEEDING TO KNOW
AND CHOOSING
TO BE STILL AND SAY
ON WHATEVER MOUNTAIN,
VALLEY,
OR RIVER
YOU ARE
BEING LED
INTO TODAY.

You stand at the base
of the mountain,
cold air swipes
the bridge of your nose.

High above,
in October,
it snows,
and at the same time,
from where you stand,
autumn burns the leaves
orange and yellow.

Here in this tension
there is no divide,
for at the mountain
there is space
for ice and light
to have their place.

It is hard to notice
beauty
on the rain-shadow side of the mountain.
You are thirsty for a spring,
even a hint of morning dew,
but you are overwhelmed by the desert
that feels like nothingness
unraveling endlessly
inside you.

Look long,
look slow,
the shadows before you
will start to grow
forward.

There is more ahead of you
that you have yet to know.

The range of the mesas rise up in the distance.

Their song is in a different tongue
than the mountains you once knew,
but oh, how beautiful their sound.
Do not be afraid
of your voice.

SOME DAYS WE'RE
THE PAINTER.
SOME DAYS WE'RE
THE PAINT.
BEAUTIFUL THINGS
ARE BEING MADE
ALL THE SAME

A building cannot stand
without understanding
the foundations.
This is a season of
waiting.

No more building up,
but rather, digging down
to discover what lies beneath,
excavating what must go
and watering what gives strength.
Here on the ground,
you wait
with soil-soaked knees,
hoping
in this earth
there is still hope
to be found.

Trust that no matter what is revealed,
Light will meet you there.

Paint chips from the staircase.
Floorboards creak beneath you.
Music plays in your mind,
the old record player still spinning its rings
in your memory.

The trips you used to take
last August at the lake.

Your single key hangs quietly from its ring.
Door closed.

Engine on.
It's time to figure out who you are.

Your heart will heal with time
as you leave this town and her sunset behind.

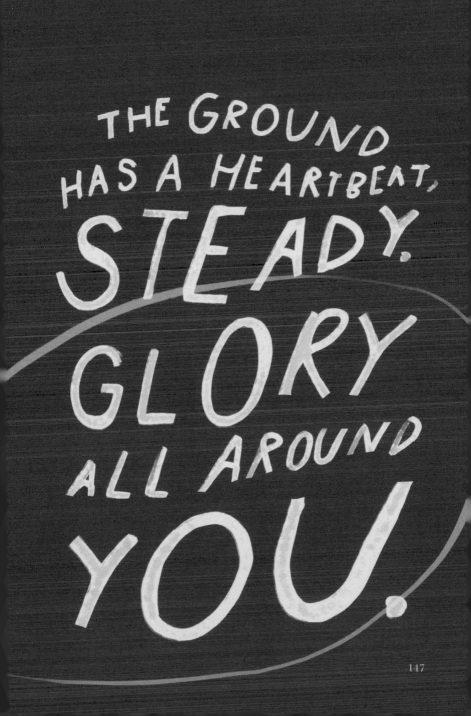

THE GROUND HAS A HEARTBEAT, STEADY. GLORY ALL AROUND YOU.

147

uly 1996.

The Texan plains go on forever, and then forever finally ends, and the west starts again with New Mexico. There was no sight of the sun yet as we left the hotel. I slid onto the cool, gray leather seats of the Volvo and struggled to pry open my eyes as we headed around the bend into downtown Albuquerque. With the windows down, at seventy miles per hour, the wind roared like water. In the pitch black, I lost myself in its sound. Who knew air could hold such power? Back home in Georgia, the wind sings, but it somehow always gets tangled in the arms of the pine trees. Out here, in New Mexico, there are no trees to hold it back. Unrestrained, the wind twisted through my fingers and made every hair on my head dance. I pressed my arm out the window, resisting the wind's throbbing pressure, and I curled my index finger to my thumb to hold a little ball of wind. I knew I couldn't take it with me, so I closed my eyes to memorize the way it felt on my skin. With every mile we traversed, the wind traveled through our car with a heavy force, a reminder in the quiet of the desert that this world is far bigger than me.

Forever. I want to remember this forever, I thought to myself. We were just passing through, another day, another journey in these hills of Albuquerque. I wanted to know: *How do you capture wind and take it with you?*

July 2016.

The wind coursed through my car once again. Decades later, she is as faithful as ever, sweeping in and out of Albuquerque with the same power and force that she showed me as a child. Traveling down this stretch of road always makes me think of my younger self. The wind carries me back to who I am. I'm very aware that this does not make sense, and I'm content with that.

As I drove, I surrendered to the beauty of the glorious Sandia Mountains climbing high around me. I looked at creation, and I saw God's majesty unfolding all around me and within me too. In the shadow of the mountains, I was reminded of my lowliness, knowing that no matter how many library books I would read, these mountains hold secret stories that I will never know. I respected them, for I knew they were much grander than me. I had never actually taken the time to stop here and explore. I was always pressing toward the next destination. Family was waiting. Work was waiting. Someone was always waiting.

I felt an impulse to get out of the car and touch the earth. I had read about the La Luz Trail, thirteen miles of rocky paths twisting around ridges, lined with green shrubbery and piñon trees. Hikers printed their footprints into the path day by day, only to be erased under night's heavy shield, as the dust and wind conspired to cover their tracks. As I sat behind the wheel of my car, I imagined myself placing the palm of my hand on the dawn-drenched face of a rock in the mountain. *Does she have a story?* I wondered. *What is her name? What has she seen? Has someone mistreated her, left her, abandoned and forgotten her with time? Have the years made her wiser and stronger?* I wanted to slow down and listen to the stories in that mountain.

I wondered how long she would be here, in all her natural beauty. The heat blazed hotter, and the cracks in the earth ran dry. She was resilient under the pressure of wind and sun, but even so, I knew she could not escape the cruelties of time. I wondered what she looked like hundreds of years ago, without wrinkles and weather-worn skin. I wondered if her trees would survive this decade. She struggled to maintain her natural beauty, under attack, with no one to defend her. Why weren't we defending her? *If I don't stop my car and pull over now, will I miss my opportunity?* These hills had seen so much and come so far, but I wondered how much more they could endure. Where would the bees go, and the other wildlife of these hills? I feared the next time I returned to New Mexico, I may no longer smell the scent of vanilla pines wafting through the wind. I wondered again, *How do you capture the wind and take it with you?*

Still, I pressed on. My drive was fast and fleeting. The wind will keep howling and we will all keep traveling and I will struggle, wondering what I can do to help. Will I ever have time to simply sit and enjoy the earth for what she is worth? I never seemed to be anywhere long enough. These questions follow me as I continue rolling down the interstate. In the end, I resolved to admire the rocks from a distance. I decided that their allure stems from their unknowability. This is what makes them sacred. I kept driving, but I vowed to commit myself to goodness. I can still do good things from afar.

On the road.

On the road.

Who knew we could fall in love with passing things?

Why, oh, why can't I seem to get close?

I chose to help in the only way I knew how—to make beautiful things. I vowed to create with the colors of the places I passed. I watched as the steel-blue sky lightened to a shade of teal. And then blue turned into blush pink, and just like that, on the tip of the horizon, I could see the sun crashing through with bright orange hues. These colors became the palette of my earliest work. In fact, when people ask about my process, there's not much I can tell them, except perhaps they should go to Albuquerque. These colors became a prism for my mind's eye. Blues and pinks from a journey up a mountain I may never hike. I dream of it, and it makes me feel connected to a beautiful world that at times feels fleeting and far away, and when I think of her sky, the words pour on the page.

So many of the beautiful moments in my life have been fleeting.

Silhouettes of mountains along the interstates.

Tangled words in my heart I was never able to say.

Friends I was just getting to know before I had to move away . . .

New Mexico reminds me that life is fleeting,

like the wind,

every moment passing by like the hills on my long drives.
All that I have missed
by never being present.
I love the mountains, but their foundations I can never
know.
I can come back here over and over, only to unfold new
unknowns.
Wind I cannot capture,
but I carry with me the color of the sky.
The slight hint of a highway sunrise.
The teal-blue lines dancing on the railing along the I-40
West ramp.

And even now, I want to go back. I want to look closer. I want to stay longer, like a child asking for five more minutes.

But as I get older, I learn that there is only so much time in my day, and New Mexico is not my place to stay. Like so many other travelers on this road, I encountered something glorious on the way. But her wind and her earth inspire me. She is steady and true, and I simply hope she will be there for me when I need her again.

THE WILD HORSE
UNDRIBLED
UNDER MOONLIGHT,
PUSHES HER WAY
INTO THE FULLNESS
OF NIGHT,
SHE RUNS TILL
SHE FLIES,
ROAMING
WITH SHOULDERS STRONG
AS THE MOUNTAIN,
UNAFRAID OF
RISING SHADOWS,
FOR THE DESERT
IS A PLACE
SHE KNOWS.

DUST RISES UP
AS SHE DANCES
UNDER THE STARS.

SHE KNOWS
BENEATH THEM,
SHE IS FREE.

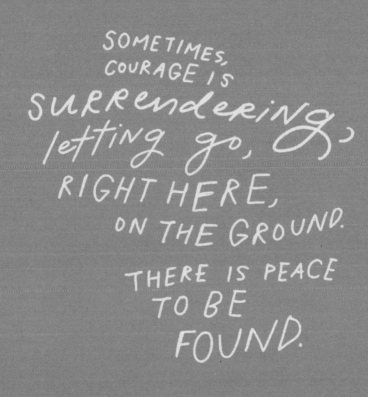

SOMETIMES, COURAGE IS SURRENDERING, letting go, RIGHT HERE, ON THE GROUND. THERE IS PEACE TO BE FOUND.

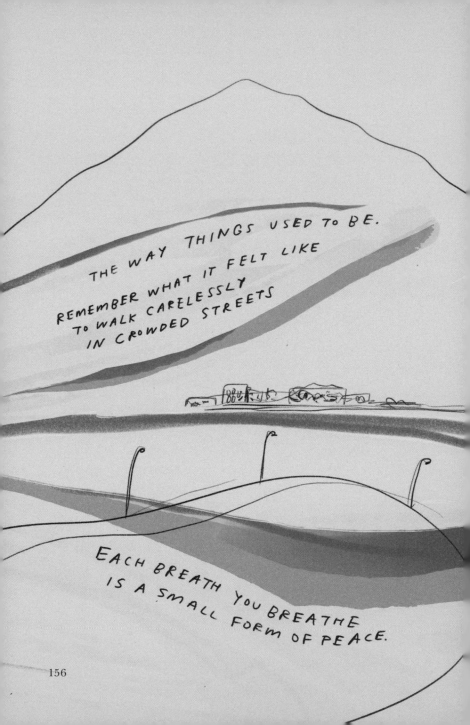

THE WAY THINGS USED TO BE.

REMEMBER WHAT IT FELT LIKE
TO WALK CARELESSLY
IN CROWDED STREETS

EACH BREATH YOU BREATHE
IS A SMALL FORM OF PEACE.

Notice the north mountain.
Not only the peaks,
but the bases beneath
dipping down into the valley,
holding still in all weather.

And every year you come back,
you have grown a little taller, wiser,
and older in your shoulders,
and yet,
you still carry
your youth,
speechless
at what is greater than you.

THE MOUNTAINS ROAR, HUMBLING US. WE ARE SO MUCH SMALLER THAN WE THINK.

Your pace is slow,
your mind is fogged.
You breathe in pine,
and every cell is set alight.
A tingling in your fingers
and a power in your toes.

On this path, you went out alone
to try something new.
There's no need to compare yourself
to those around you.

Promises made and promises broken,
painful patterns and hard red rocks—
carrying sorrow.
You fear what lies ahead tomorrow.

Will the wind rush off
and take the red away?
When I return, will it all be gray?
Will rivers turn to flat beds
of cracked, scorched earth?

Will butterflies still fly,
and if not, how will I?

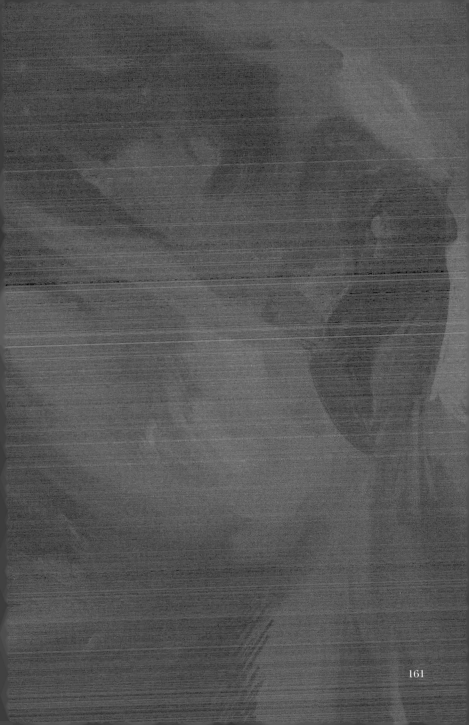

As you hike
through this canyon,
these layers of earth
laid one on another,
year upon year
stacked high into the heavens
and carved down by wind and water,
it may take time
to comprehend the majesty.
Notice the blues
and oranges
and feel them on your skin.
Words cannot capture this.

As you breathe
in the subtle, sweet scent
from the red bark
of the ponderosa pines,
you are free to do nothing at all.
Just notice what's before you.
Oh, the glory of surrender.

For perhaps what is grand
is not meant to be understood,
and to truly see
what you are meant to see
requires a slow softening
of your heart.

Remember.
Trust that after all
you lost and all it cost,
you are not finished yet.
You are filled
with the beauty
of that sunset.
And as you feel your heart hasten,
I hope you are reminded
even in the stillness,
when you feel small,
you are invited to stand tall
between these walls of sand,
each particle much smaller than you.

INHALE, EXHALE.
NEVER FORGET
THE GREEN LIGHTS,
STOP SIGNS
AND HIGHWAYS
THAT BROUGHT YOU HERE,
EVERY SINGLE STEP ACCOUNTED FOR.
EVEN THOUGH YOU CAN'T SEE
WHERE THE ROAD LEADS,
WHAT MATTERS IS THAT YOU TRAVEL
NOT IN PURSUIT OF KNOWING IT ALL
BUT IN PURSUIT OF BOUNDLESS PEACE

IN THE WILD OF CHANGING WINDS, MY HEART IS SLOUCHED TOWARD HOPE. EVEN THOUGH I STILL HAVE A THOUSAND MILES TO GO, I WILL HONOR THE GROUND BENEATH ME.

167

The air grows colder as you climb farther north. You
join the company of ponderosa pines lining the road.
Coconino Plateau. You have fifty-four miles to go.
The trees start to sing. Their green leaves sway into a
song that seems as if it is just for you.
Welcome to this new unknown.
Be surprised by where.
Welcome to this new unknown.
Let the harmonies surprise you.
Let your voice echo out
into this heavenly choir
and let your melody shift and grow
into all the octaves of yourself.

GRAND CANYON TRIP, 1996

THE TIRES MOVE
BENEATH YOUR FEET,
ROLLING OVER ENDLESS CONCRETE
THEY ROLL ROUND AND
ROUND AGAIN.
UNRESTRAINED BY
ROCKS OR CLAY OR WIND
BUT EVENTUALLY PUNCTURED
AND RUN TOO THIN.
NEVERTHELESS,
THEY SPIN FORWARD,
COVERING GROUND
AS LONG AS THEY CAN
IN THIS CONTINUAL
RHYTHMIC AND PURPOSED.

Oh, how the wild marigold grows
even when highway travelers pass her by.
She grows amongst the others
and still has a particular way she shines.
Few notice her
from where they stand.
They do not see her ochre brushstrokes

painted on the canvas of the desert.

When the sun slips out
of the sky,
she is hidden
all the more
under the masterpiece
of a star-filled night.
And still by night, she stretches high.
There is wholeness to her store.
No matter who does
or does not notice,
she still unfolds
with courage.

The final few hundred miles of interstate stretched out before us like the yellow brick road, only there was no Emerald City; there were no lush green trees or scarecrows to greet us along the way. We were just a family of four from Georgia, faithfully headed to California in a Volvo with no air-conditioning, overcome by an orange desert heat whipping through our windows.

This was the first big trip we had ever taken. Living on a pastor's income, we didn't have the funds to travel often. It wasn't until I was much older that I realized some families take vacations annually, and they often adventured to high-rise cities or set out on lavish cruises. But still, our humble journey meant everything to me. The one-story motels, truck stops, and fast-food drive-throughs may not have compared to a trip to Disney World or a resort on a distant island, but that didn't matter to us. We were a family that knew how to have fun, and old-fashioned road trips were good enough for us.

Somewhere between the western edge of New Mexico and the "Welcome to Arizona" state sign, my sister and I turned to the back seat to find our only set of crayons, which we had set aside somewhere back on the west side of Texas, was frying like an egg in the window under the piercing desert sun. I reached out to recover the colorful hot wax blaze, only to discover that despite its alluring hues, it was as hot as a cast-iron skillet on a stove. I recoiled, devastated at the loss. We still had quite a long way to go on our journey, and now our last activity was melting away before our eyes.

I blew on my blistering finger and watched helplessly as the melted crayons muddled together. It was all too familiar. As a child with dyslexia, I hardly had a moment where the words on pages or billboards or road signs did not get jumbled together in some way. I loved to read and write, but it often took me longer than everyone else to find my words. So I drew pictures instead. Shapes and colors were the bridges between my thoughts and what I couldn't seem to figure out how to say.

When the Arizona heat raged against the car window, I saw orange.

When the radio signal dropped in the mountains, my mind went white.

When the tires rattled over a pothole, everything was bright red.

The colors were my words. And now they were muddled too.

I still had a few pages in my little notebook to fill, and I desperately tried to rescue whatever was left of the crayons from the pool of wax in the back window. I pulled them out of the sun's direct rays, and after a few moments, I gathered them in my hands. I absorbed their heat into my palms and watched how the yellows, oranges, reds melted together into brown, the color of my skin. I tried to press the colors onto the page, but the wax dried before I could do anything with it.

"Oh, look, we're almost there . . ."

I looked up to see a sign outside the window. It moved past us like lightning, but I assumed it meant we were getting closer to the Grand Canyon. As we pulled into the park, I struggled to read sign after sign brimming with too many words, and we passed them before I could comprehend what they said. I bit my lip, frustrated with myself because I felt like I was missing important information.

I was tired of missing the signs. I was wary in these moments because I was not able to read fast enough. I felt out of control. Were they displaying words of warning or secrets of the earth? What was I missing? These unknown words assaulted every fiber of curiosity within me. If only the words were a little bigger or a little bolder, then I could make sense of the signs like the grown-ups.

Finally, we parked, and we all stumbled out of our car to capture a glimpse of this ancient wonder on our cameras so we could take it home with us. The sun slid closer toward the earth, and the ponderosa pines cast long shadows, like a ballerina stretching at the end of a long day's dance. I skipped ahead, in front of my sister and parents. I tried to wait for them to catch up, but my light-up sneakers seemed to carry me forward all on their own.

In just a few short skips, I found myself at the edge of the earth, and I immediately grabbed on to the wooden guardrail to peer into the canyon below. The sharp-edged rock face softened into a honey-colored horizon under a slowly fading golden sun. Its depths were beyond my imagination. I watched as the sun's final rays peered in sideways, revealing layers of earth that went on for miles and miles. The sky and the earth were in some sort of wordless dance, and I was their spectator, awestruck and grateful. Everything else melted away, except the colors. Who knew the earth could create so many colors?

And then my attention shifted to the thin layer of crayon wax still coating my fingers. I slowly pressed my hands together, studying the dance of the yellow and orange lumps, each piece bearing my fingerprint as it curled away from my skin. I rubbed my hands faster, watching one color bleed into the next, and before I knew it, the colors seemed to move through me, sinking deep into my pores. Here on the edge of the earth, I held the sunset in my hands—my own molten masterpiece. I looked back to the fiery canyon below, the hot winds pouring through those layers of sand, delicately ironed together through the centuries. What a grand creation, indeed.

After days of truck horns and crinkling hamburger wrappers and garish radio personalities, we now stood in silence, with only the wind to serenade us. Just the four of us, in complete stillness. In awe of it all, my mom answered, in a low, pure tone:

Then sings my soul
My Savior God to Thee
How great Thou art
How great Thou art.

I felt the words beneath the music. And beneath the music, I felt silence. A colorful, radiant silence that invited me just to be, without having to worry about reading or writing or making sense of anything. The glory of the earth was beyond my comprehension. Language could not do this justice.

Finally, the sunset faded from the sky, and the park closed under the rule of darkness. Other parents shuffled their children into their minivans. "That was so cool!" "What's for dinner?" "I have to go to the bathroom!" The voices of other kids tugged at my ears, shaking me back down to the ground from the sky filled with color. We loaded into the Volvo, and before I knew it, we were back on the interstate making the final trek to California. Music blasted from the car stereos, and the truck horns reverberated in the air, and we drove on in darkness.

But I knew I would always remember that moment at the canyon's edge. This was the first time I felt connected without having to read, write, or speak a single word. Nature doesn't speak in highway signs or sonnets. And I realized maybe I didn't have to either. Colors on my hand, colors on my skin—this was my language, and I didn't have to apologize for that. I felt free.

When the sun returned the following morning, I asked my parents if we could stop to buy a new set of crayons, because I knew I had more to draw, more to say. The canyons and the crayons taught me that beauty is all around us, if we're willing to invite it in. I was determined that, like the canyon and the light, I too would make beautiful things, wordlessly, in my own way. And so I colored and colored and colored again. Then sings *my* soul.

A NOTE TO
SIX YEAR OLD ME:
I KNOW
IT'S SO HARD
FOR YOU
TO PUT THE
WORDS TOGETHER...
YOU STRUGGLE
WITH THE FORM
THE STRUCTURE
AND THE LETTERS,
BUT
THE WAY YOU SEE COLOR
AND HEAR MUSIC
IS A PART OF YOUR SOUL.

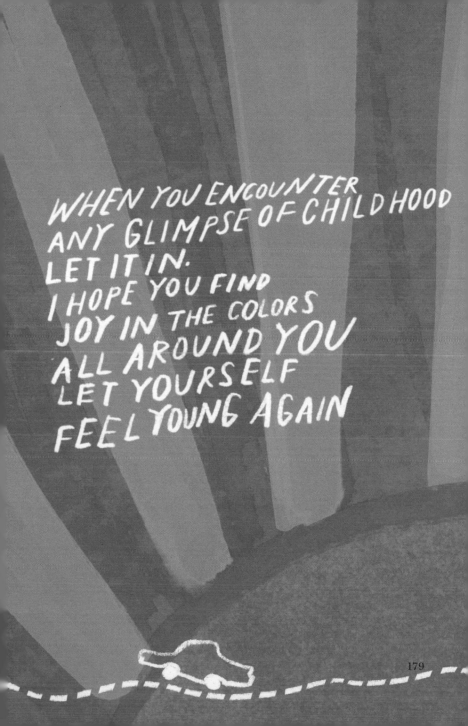

WHEN YOU ENCOUNTER
ANY GLIMPSE OF CHILDHOOD
LET IT IN.
I HOPE YOU FIND
JOY IN THE COLORS
ALL AROUND YOU
LET YOURSELF
FEEL YOUNG AGAIN

I HOPE YOU KNOW HOW MUCH IT MATTERS THAT
YOU HAVE NOT GIVEN UP,
EVEN THOUGH YOU HOLD
PERSISTENT FEARS
THAT YOU ARE NOT GOOD ENOUGH.
YOU HAVE GIVEN YOUR ALL
WITH COURAGE.
YOU HAVE LEARNED TO REST AND TRUST.
YOUR STORY IS LINED WITH HEALING AND HOPE.
OH, WHAT LIGHT STIRS TO LIFE
FROM THE DUST!

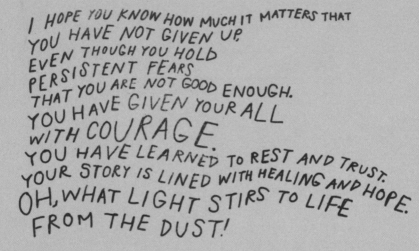

The hours pass slowly in the desert
as you watch the cacti's silhouette
stretch
inch by inch
across the ground
with every minute
by minute.
The sun presses you against the scorching earth,
and you see orange haze rippling in the wind.
The earth rises all around you like a tidal wave.
You cannot escape the hot winds
finding their way to your skin.
Let yourself awaken,
heart open,
shoulders loose.
Keep your knees steady,
lift your chin,
and look up to see
where the Light pours in.

In the quiet desert,
I am slowing down.
I am learning how to trust
Light's song
here in the dust.

The wind's whistle pierces my ear,
but beneath her shrill cries
I hear the pounding rhythm to the land
pulsing beneath my feet.
And the longer I stand still
her pounding reminds me
of the melody
that plays
in the room between my ribs
holding
my heart beat.

In the emptiness,
I feel strong.
I am leaning into
silence
and I am listening.

For even the rocks
are fully present,
as dust scatters off to
waltz with the wind.
They are set here
in an endless dance,
revealing majesty.

Down here
in the desert
in the quiet,
Light meets me on the ground.

May my soul
stay attuned
to hear
that sacred ground.

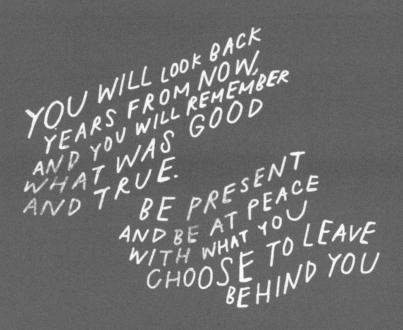

YOU WILL LOOK BACK
YEARS FROM NOW,
AND YOU WILL REMEMBER
WHAT WAS GOOD
AND TRUE.

BE PRESENT
AND BE AT PEACE
WITH WHAT YOU
CHOOSE TO LEAVE
BEHIND YOU

Let your weakness
be the wellspring
of your wonder.
Let the gaps
between the rocks
becomes spaces
where you are free
to bring courage to life
and become who you
were meant to be.

Come out of the wasteland,
come and rest by the water.
You are not a faceless traveler,
you are Beloved,
you are Daughter.
Notice how the waves push their way
over thousands of miles
right here, to the soles
of your tired feet.
Notice how,
even though you are not
sure how you got here,
you no longer question
if you were meant to be.

No longer hiding,
only abiding
out in the open,
no longer ashamed.
And in the stillness,
just listen,
please listen.
Hear the ocean
call your name.

May the questions you are living with today
slow down into the sweetest reverie,
a flow of life, a dream.

Focus not on the quantity of your thoughts
or fears whether your words provoke
profundity.

Let your questions of significance fall down
into the well of grace,
for within it, every part of your restless mind
and every beat of your heavy heart has its place,
and you are enough.

Palm trees
with arms open wide
adorn our shore with pride.
They come from everywhere across the seven seas—
from western Sonora, the queen palm,
from Queensland, the king palm,
the date palm of Africa's northern rim,
the date palm from the Canaries,
and here, their roots
grow deep
together
to bear one another.

LIKE A
BRIGHT YELLOW KITE
FIGHTING HER WAY
THROUGH
THE WIND,
EVEN WHEN
YOU FEEL
DISTANT,
YOU ARE
STILL
TETHERED AT
THE OTHER
END

YOU ARE NOT OUT OF TIME

SOFTEN YOUR HEART
AND FEEL THE WATER
ON YOUR SKIN

The evening sun
suspends over the blue,
mixing salmon pink
and starfish orange
into its topwater hues.
The earthy fragrance of
the kelp beds
awakens your heart.
As the sky transforms
into the dark,
you choose to open your heart
to boundless living too.

THE MORE I SURRENDER MY NEED TO SUCCEED, THE MORE I CAN SEE WHAT WAS FOR ME.

On that cold morning, scaled gray,
when you awake
in the middle of an unknown sea,
overwhelmed by breaking waves
and the silence in between,
remember how calm
a body of water can be,
and even when
new waves unfold
and you lose control,
trust this is not forever.

And in all those spaces of your heart
where you have been wrecked
working hard
to build up strength
to fight the length
of long weary days like this,

you are free
to be undone
under this cloud-covered sun
underneath
this blanket overcast.

Time will pass
and at last
you will remember,
you will remember
what your soul has long known:
in all of this unfolding
you are still on
a journey
home.

*P*alm trees lined the street, standing tall and orderly, like guards awaiting a queen. Their green hats brushed against a clear blue sky, and their long, narrow bodies stood at attention, stretching tall toward the heavens. My parents rushed ahead mindlessly, as parents do, completely oblivious to the solemnity of the moment. I let go of my mother's hand and stood back, drawn in by the trees' dignity. A dew drop fell from one of the fronds and rested on my lip, an enticing appetizer to break my fast on this Sunday morning. Its saltiness awakened my mind to the sea only a few miles away, and a cold chill rushed through my body at the thought of the sea breeze that awaited me. I froze in my tracks, wide-awake, watching the palm branches swaying in the wind. *Are they waving at me?*

"Come on, Morgan, everyone's waiting on us."

I rushed through the palm tree procession to the stucco building at the end of the street. My father would be preaching this morning just beyond these wooden doors, which looked like they had been carved from the California redwoods I'd seen in my books. I noticed the rings in their grain, knowing that each bump and crevice held stories from hundreds of years ago. Oh, I wished they could speak and tell me of all they had seen, but they kept their secrets quiet. Iron bolts secured the doors open, inviting those passing by to step into a kingdom of grace just beyond these walls. All stories were welcome here.

Beautiful women adorned with fuchsia and violet hats stood inside the entrance, with "Good mornings" and "How are yous" and even a "My, don't you look lovely." I entered the hall to find dim, yellow lights shining on an organ bellowing in the background while a choir in crimson robes found their seats at the front. I looked up at the stained-glass window and noticed the sun casting her colorful beams throughout the room. It was enchanting, to be sure, but my mind continued to race with the calling of the palm trees outside. I was caught in daydreams of the beach and surfing and sea turtles waddling in the sand.

I'd recently become obsessed with sea turtles. Their beautiful shells always captivated me when I read about them in my encyclopedia. They're recluses while at sea, but once a year, they return to the shore in droves. They're bold right from birth, emerging from their egg shells all by themselves, breaking through carefully and slowly. And shortly after, they waddle their way toward the ocean, knowing they were made for those salt waves. The journey into the depths is a trial for the little ones, and they face endless challenges as they grow and go with the flow of life. I would imagine the smallest one, bobbing her little head, drifting under her rounded shell, in the water. In my mind's eye, I saw her wide eyes staring back at me, unaware of the dangerous currents that awaited her. She would journey far beyond the shore for many miles, all alone. She'd travel into uncertainty, and when nesting season returned, she would gather the courage to travel wave over wave to where she began on shore. Like her mother before her, she would always find her way back home.

"Oh, you're one of the preacher's daughters, right?"

My eyes were locked on the stained-glass window just over her orange hat.

"Um . . . yes."

My stomach tightened as I realized I should have said more. With all of the colors filling my eyes, I was struggling to focus. I worried she thought I was rude.

From a young age, as a preacher's daughter, I felt the burden of unrealistic expectations. People expected perfection or rebellion. But I belonged to a rarely mentioned third category—the curious but never-quite-sure-where-they-fit, never-quite-feeling-equipped category. The girl who wanted to sing, but the song got trapped in her lungs, so she chose the piano instead, but her fingers still failed to find the right patterns of the music. The girl whose speech could never match the brightness of her yellow dress, no matter how much she tried. The girl who simply wasn't interested in meeting new people every single week, peppering them with mundane questions of their workdays or the weather.

I wasn't like my mom or my sister, who thrived under the attention. Everyone in my family seemed to scatter to every corner of the church, ebbing and flowing in and out of conversations, laughing, speaking, and sharing in an occasional hearty *amen* with someone they had just met. They'd meet and greet and wear bright pinks and greens, and they had the personalities to match it. They would burst into song, even where there was no music. Even my father—*the preacher*—was a drummer. He was a master of words at the pulpit, but he also worked beyond words, filling the air with the rhythms of his bass drum and snare, leading the whole congregation in unity.

Meanwhile, as I stood there in church, I struggled to clap. I couldn't hear my voice. I couldn't find my beat with my feet against this burgundy carpet. And when the song was over, my hands were left pink with a hot sting from trying so hard. The music was riotous, but I was not part of it. I felt stuck on the shore, like a newborn sea turtle left behind by the others who were heading out to enjoy the salty sea.

The choir members took their seats, and my dad walked to

the pulpit. I didn't enjoy having a spotlight cast on me, but I loved watching my dad preach. I loved my dad. He has always had a talent for speaking, but at his core, he is more reserved, like me. I remember days when I would crawl up in his lap at my childhood home and watch him write his sermon notes in a black leather-bound notebook, each row of text crafted in perfectly straight lines and capital letters. Pages and pages of research, questions, and thoughts, scribbled in a rich blue ink filling the pages like paint on a canvas. Whenever he spoke, I imagined his words filling the room in streaks of blue.

As he began to preach, I pulled out my reliable black-and-white composition notebook. This was my safe space to find my own voice, and I'd try to write my own notes just like my father's. I didn't have a fancy blue pen like his, so I settled for a pencil. Someday, I hoped, maybe I'd write something worthy of blue ink, but I knew, not yet.

From his podium, bathed in all the colors of the window, Dad asked us to turn to the book of Psalms. I wrote down the verse as best as I could, but before I could get too far, I noticed my p was already backward. I was frustrated, but I figured it was better to write something on the page rather than nothing. I switched to drawing instead. Dad talked about King David, and the courage he mustered even as he stood scared and alone as a young kid. I drew this young man with his robe and straggly beard and all of the men and women around him. I drew the battles he fought, and the people he loved, and the procession of trees I imagined welcoming him home to the place he belonged. I held in my hands the picture of a man making mistakes and living day by day, just doing his best to live out his life in the way he was meant to. Occasionally, one of Dad's words would catch my ear, and I'd tuck its letters into the drawing as best as I could, backward or forward. I did my best to capture the life of this David—a young man out of place but brave nonetheless.

My creative trance was finally broken by the sound of the choir, drawing out joy with every breath. I wasn't finished with my drawing yet, but I knew the congregation's eyes were on me. I couldn't be caught drawing in church, not as a preacher's daughter. I closed the notebook.

After church, we headed back to my grandmother's house, where we were staying for the next few days. Slumping into a Sunday stupor, the entire family spread out around the house, flopping on couches and dozing off into naps. While everyone else was resting or chatting around the dinner table, I tucked away to a corner of the living room to review my work from earlier that morning. I noticed my dad resting on the couch, the likely next victim of the Sunday nap. He no longer wore his tie and jacket, but I always felt he was most dignified when he was like this. Fully approachable, a bit tired, and finally finding rest after a long week of travel and preparation.

I looked at the gray and white smudges on the pages in my hand, embarrassed and a little ashamed, and while I knew there was still work to be done, I felt an uncontrollable impulse to be in my dad's lap and show him what I had made. I strolled over and nuzzled myself into his arms, casually opening my notebook and hoping he would say something about the drawing before him. My heart started beating faster, suddenly aware of just how many mistakes covered this page. My notebook certainly couldn't compare to his perfectly penned blue script. I wasn't worthy of the same acclaim he received every week from that pulpit.

Without words, I slid my notebook into my dad's line of

vision. He looked and he smiled. I let out a breath I didn't know I was holding. I wondered what he was thinking, since I couldn't imagine how he could make sense of my sloppy sheet of notes and doodles. But still, he was smiling.

"God created you to create."

I looked down and tried to see what he saw. I looked up to ask him, but before I could say anything, he put his hand on my shoulder. And it was then I noticed that there were tears in his eyes.

"I can see that this is coming from your heart."

I looked back down at the page and now I could see a blue color in David's robe, a crimson-colored cloud of dust behind the army, green pastures, and a golden sun.

I never stopped drawing. From then on, I doodled and colored and painted. Nothing could stop me from creating, because this was my calling. This was my heart poured out on the page. And my dad liked it, so who else did I need to please?

I sat on my grandmother's porch for the rest of the day, knowing we would have to leave soon. Our trip to California went by too quickly, and I knew we wouldn't get to the shore before we had to make the long journey back home. I tasted the air and listened to the sound of seagulls, trying to soak in every bit of the coast into my pores before we had to go.

"One day I'll be back. I just know it. One day I'll reach those blue waves."

Twenty years passed, and in all that time, I never made it back.

But then, in my mid-twenties, my mom's chronic illness started to worsen. She and my dad traveled back to California for a few months to meet with some new doctors in hopes that

someone could find answers to alleviate her pain. There were no easy answers, but they decided to take the plunge and move west to help her. With nothing to lose, my husband and I decided to join them. My sister came as well. Like the sea turtles I had imagined waddling along the shore, here we were, family members scattered far and wide returning to California together all these years later. I always knew I would return to the West Coast, but I never could have imagined these circumstances.

I dragged the last box through the sand outside, up the steps, and into the living room. I opened up the first box of my own belongings and stumbled upon my stationery. I had since graduated from the black-and-white composition books I loved as a kid, but I was still a sucker for crisp, blank pages in a brand-new journal. As I touched the blank page, my memory of that Sunday afternoon in the front pew came to my mind. I felt like a kid again. I remembered how my dad spoke so lovingly to me and how he believed in me when I didn't yet believe in myself. I remembered the blue pens I prized and realized it was time to meet the shores I'd dreamed of all those years before.

I grabbed the car keys and followed the ocean breeze to find my way to the shore. I drove through streets lined with orange trees, with fruits adorning their branches like the brightly colored hats of church ladies from years past. I knew if these trees could speak, they would greet me just the same. They made me feel like a queen finally coming home.

I pulled into the parking lot and sprung from the driver's seat with nothing more than a No. 2 pencil and some blank sheets of paper. I raced to the boardwalk and hovered over the water, listening to her cascading rhythms and watching her waves crest with white peaks. Oh, the water was wide and vast, unforgiving in her might and soothing in her roar. She humbled me. To think of all the life out there, an ecosystem behaving in perfect harmony, each living thing doing the work it was called to do.

I imagined looking down to the shore and dreamed once again of that baby turtle, gently making her way to the water, wide-eyed and brave for whatever she may face. I imagined she too was looking for the home where she knew she belonged. I supposed the ocean's blue was calling her too.

I lifted my pencil to sketch her. In all capital letters, I wrote the words *IT IS WELL*. I was still working with plain charcoal, but over the years, I had learned to see the blues, greens, and golds as possibilities. I looked out to the calmness of the sea and the golden warmth of the sun oozing down into the air above me.

Beauty all around me. I did not have to sing or speak or write a single sentence to know that something was still stirring from within my heart, and with scratched-through letters and elementary sketches, this was my home, and I could still make art.

SIT WITH WORDS AND STAND ON THEM

Water
feels soft
in the morning rain.

Each drop
is a wordless beckoning
to come awake
out of our sleep.
We travel outward,
into the busy world
in raincoats or
under umbrellas,
but even within this armor,
we cannot escape rain's invitation
as it taps into the puddles
beneath our feet.

Clouds cover the light,
but in our reflection on the pavement,
we see the rainwater
tempting us
to dance.

The blue whales
still go south in the summer.
The monarch butterflies
still journey west,
sweeping along
the southern California coast
to the mountains of Mexico,
every year,
finding home
in more than one place.

You were never alone
whether moving
or sitting still.
It is well
in your well-traveled soul.

become a kid again.
engage the process
of unfolding
and holding
all the things that
make us who we are.

rearrange them
into ### letters,
recipes,
;IDEAS;—
MAKE YOUR
ART

211

Here in the city,
you lift your weary head
and bathe in the Light.
With your feet on the ground
you slowly lay down
your freshly picked
palm leaf,
preparing your heart
to welcome Peace,
who meets you
in your lowest place,

the belonging
your heart
has always craved.

MORNING CLOUDS
DESCEND
TO MASK THE
REDWOOD'S
BLUSHING SKIN.
A SISTERHOOD
OF TREES,
THEY
GROW
AND
GROW.
THE
WORLD
IS QUIET
HERE
AND
NO ONE
IS
ALONE.

Redwood National Park

213

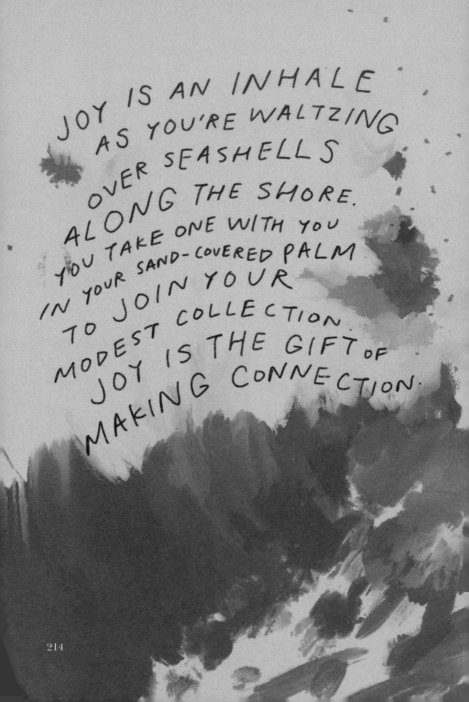

JOY IS AN INHALE
AS YOU'RE WALTZING
OVER SEASHELLS
ALONG THE SHORE.
YOU TAKE ONE WITH YOU
IN YOUR SAND-COVERED PALM
TO JOIN YOUR
MODEST COLLECTION.
JOY IS THE GIFT OF
MAKING CONNECTION.

THOUGH
MY WORRIES
CLIMB HIGH
UP THE WALLS
OF WATER
ON EITHER SIDE
OF ME,
I MUST REMEMBER
THE PATH
BENEATH
MY FEET.

I IMAGINE
HOW THE SEA
MAY COME
CRASHING DOWN
ON ME,
BUT I MUST TRUST
I WILL BE GUIDED.

I want to look back on my life
and say,
I lived in surrender.
Light found me on the road,
tired and burdened,
and I learned to let go,
learning to live beyond my history
embracing mystery,
loving the map of where I've been
and loving my questions even more
because the questions kept me
trusting
the journey home
was worth living for.